LOCOMOTIVE

BRIAN SOLOMON

MBI Publishing Company

DEDICATION

In the memory of my grandmother, Bessie Solomon

———————◆———————

First published in 2001 by MBI Publishing Company, Galtier Plaza, Suite 200, 380 Jackson Street, St. Paul, MN 55101-3885 USA

MBI Publishing Company books are also available at discounts in bulk quantity for industrial or sales-promotional use. For details write to Special Sales Manager at Motorbooks International Wholesalers & Distributors, Galtier Plaza, Suite 200, 380 Jackson Street, St. Paul, MN 55101-3885 USA

Library of Congress Cataloging-in-Publication Data Available

ISBN 0-7603-0996-5

On the front cover: The morning sun glints on the rods of Boston & Maine 494, a typical 4-4-0 American type. *Brian Solomon*

On the endpaper: A detailed study of the crosshead and lead driving wheel on Nickel Plate Road No. 765. *Brian Solomon.*

On the frontispiece: Steam-era-style class lamps and boxy number boards are featured on Battenkill Railroad 605, an Alco RS-3 diesel. *Brian Solomon*

On the title page: Green Mountain Railway GP9 1850 leads the North Walpole-to-Rutland freight XR-1 through Cavendish, Vermont, on November 2, 1993. *Brian Solomon*

On the back cover: In March 1997, three Electro-Motive SD40T-2s lead an empty potash train down the Cane Creek Branch in central Utah. *Brian Solomon*

Edited by Josh Leventhal

Designed by Two Poppie's Design

Printed in China

CONTENTS

ACKNOWLEDGMENTS   6

INTRODUCTION 8

THE STEAM LOCOMOTIVE 10
   THE AMERICAN STANDARD 12
   BOSTON & MAINE CLASS B-15 MOGUL 16
   FORNEY TANK 20
   CHICAGO & NORTH WESTERN R-1 24
   THE 0-6-0 SWITCHER 28
   NICKEL PLATE ROAD BERKSHIRE 32
   NEW YORK CENTRAL HUDSON 38
   UNION PACIFIC BIG BOY 42
   READING T-1 46
   PENNSYLVANIA T1 50

DIESEL POWER 54
   ELECTRO-MOTIVE F-UNIT 56
   ALCO "S" SWITCHERS 62
   ALCO RS-3 66
   BALDWIN'S SHARKS 70
   ALCO PA 74
   ELECTRO-MOTIVE GP9 78
   GENERAL ELECTRIC U25B 84
   ELECTRO-MOTIVE GP40 90
   MONTREAL LOCOMOTIVE WORKS SIX MOTOR LOCOMOTIVES 96
   ELECTRO-MOTIVE TUNNEL MOTORS 102
   GENERAL ELECTRIC C30-7A 108
   GENERAL ELECTRIC DASH 9 114
   ELECTRO-MOTIVE SD70MAC 118
   EMD CLASS 66 124
   GENERAL ELECTRIC AC6000CW 128

ELECTRIC LOCOMOTIVES 132
   NEW YORK CENTRAL S-MOTOR 134
   PENNSYLVANIA GG1 138
   LITTLE JOE ELECTRICS 144
   AEM-7 148
   ACELA EXPRESS 152

BIBLIOGRAPHY 158
INDEX 159

uring the course of my study of locomotives, I have met many interesting and knowledgeable people who have assisted me along the way. Many of them helped in the preparation of this book through their insights, technical knowledge, and photographs. The field of locomotives is so broad that no one individual could ever claim to be a total locomotive expert and retain any credibility. But there are certainly experts on various specific elements of locomotive knowledge. The scope of the locomotive encompasses every piece of equipment used to haul trains since the earliest days of the railways. Whenever possible I turn to those with greater or more precise knowledge than my own. It seems no locomotive is too obscure, nor any element of locomotive technology too technical or too arcane, to have avoided scrutiny. I have done my best to seek out the facts on each locomotive and present them in a logical yet interesting fashion. I have also tried to illustrate each type with interesting and compelling photographs. Many of these images are my own, or those of my father, Richard Jay Solomon, while others were exposed by fellow photographers.

A number of people made invaluable contributions. Thanks to Robert A. Buck for access to his photo collection and for his discussions and inspirations. Bob has been watching locomotives pass the window of his house since he was old enough to stand, and in 70 years has not lost his enthusiasm for the subject. George C. Corey has had the opportunity to photograph a great many locomotives and has been kind enough to share his knowledge and photographs on many occasions. Stanwood K. Bolton provided some wonderful photographs. Paul Carver offered his expertise and perspective. George S. Pitarys has been generous with his photographs and in helping track down caption information, as well as giving me the inspiration to photograph operations on the Cape Breton & Central Nova Scotia, and Quebec Cartier lines. Thanks to Bill Linley for his help in Nova Scotia. Special thanks to the employees of Quebec Cartier for their hospitality.

H. Bentley Crouch was kind to let me peruse his vast collection of railway photographs, and assisted with photo captioning. Dennis LeBeau lent me prints from the William Bullard Archive, and shared his enthusiasm for photography and the Boston & Albany. Doug Moore assisted with copywork. Brian L. Jennison provided insight on the Southern Pacific, and accompanied me on many photographic excursions. Likewise, Tom Hoover has spent many years sharing his enthusiasm for modern diesel locomotives. Tom Danneman lent his contagious enthusiasm for the Burlington Northern and the SD70MAC. Tim Doherty allowed me access to his photography and photo collection, and encouraged me to ride the inaugural *Acela Express*. Patrick Yough helped in tracking down technical information and provided insight on photo locations. Mike Gardner helped in many ways. In addition to accompanying me on numerous photographic adventures, he has given me unrestricted access to his darkroom, and his wife, Linda, cooked many wonderful meals during the course of my printing.

Jay Williams provided many fine black-and-white photographs, as did J. R. Quinn, and Bob's Photos. Dr. Richard Leonard provided a wonderful photograph of a Big Boy in action. Both John Gruber and Mel Patrick freely supplied photographs, visual insight, and criticism; provided lodging during photographic excursions; and accompanied me on railroad trips from time to time. William D. Middleton provided inspiration by authoring *When the Steam Railroads Electrified*, which has been on my father's shelf for as long as I can remember. I have had the pleasure of reviewing his wonderful photos for inclusion in this book. Thanks to Tessa Bold, who unwittingly accompanied me on a few railroad photography trips, and found it curious when I made photos of an EWS Class 66 at Bath. Doug Eisele has been generous with his own photographs and those in his collection; in addition, he has spent many hours with me in pursuit of photographs, and given me the opportunity to see Alco diesels at work.

Thanks to the Irish Railway Records Society for the use of its comprehensive railway library. My brother, Seán Solomon, has helped indirectly in many ways during the years. My father lent his extensive library, provided numerous photographs, drove me around as a child to see GG1 electrics and other locomotives, and proofread some of the text. My mother, Maureen Solomon, tolerated these enterprises admirably, and even accompanied us on an excursion to Sunnyside Yard in Queens to photograph the GG1 4876 many years ago.

—Brian Solomon

ACKNOWLEDGMENTS

Chicago & North Western R-1 No. 456 crossing Lake Monona at Madison, Wisconsin, with a train for the Monfort Branch in January 1949.
William D. Middleton

INTRODUCTION

The compelling power of the locomotive has intrigued people for generations. From the first primitive steam engines of the early nineteenth century to the enormously powerful and extraordinarily fast machines of today, locomotives have captivated the imagination of the media, historians, and the general public. When Amtrak's high-speed *Acela Express* debuted in 2000 it made international news. The locomotive is more than a simple machine, it is an important part of American heritage. The power of the locomotive helped shape America. The locomotive and the railroads developed heavy industry on the East Coast; they played a deciding role in the Civil War; encouraged settlement in the Midwest; and forged a vital link to the Far West. In May 1869, two locomotives touched pilot to pilot at Promontory, Utah, and symbolically joined East and West. The journey across the American continent that had taken months to complete could suddenly be accomplished in just a few days. The imprint of the locomotive on America is indelible. Canada too, owes its heritage to the power of the locomotive. The great Canadian Pacific Railway was a fundamental unifying element in Canada's history.

The locomotive has taken a multitude of forms and shapes; it has been built to hundreds, if not thousands, of different designs. To many, the locomotive is exemplified by the classic steam-powered designs of the mid-nineteenth century. The 4-4-0 American type in particular is something of a locomotive archetype, a pivotal player in the nation's development and growth. Yet, the American type is just one kind of engine, among a host of different steam locomotive designs. And the steam locomotive, which for almost a century was synonymous with the railroad itself, is just one of several fundamental types of railroad motive power.

Locomotives are divided into three basic categories: steam, diesel, and electric—although the electric locomotive, as we call it, is not really a locomotive at all, but a motor. In the early days many electrified railroads referred to their electrics properly as "motors." At that time everyone knew that a locomotive was steam powered, so there was little confusion. But terminology changes with the times, and sometimes develops contradictory descriptions. So today we tend to call electrics, "electric locomotives," to distinguish them from steam and diesel designs.

Each of the basic locomotive varieties has a great number of different types, models, and manufacturers. The great variation of locomotive designs is one of the things that has made them so fascinating over the years. America has the most diverse and colorful locomotive history of any nation in the world. This is a result of the enormous number of different railroads, each with its own locomotive agenda, and of many different manufacturers. In the steam era, each railroad worked with the builders to come up with individual designs to meet specialized traffic needs. Many railroads had dozens of different types, and some had dozens of classes and subclasses of a particular type. Even the characteristics that defined a particular class varied from line to line. Electrics were never as numerous as either steam or diesel locomotives, but they were every bit as eclectic as steam in classification. Diesels, by contrast, were largely produced to standard designs decided by the manufacturers. While this reduced the sheer number of different models, the different paint schemes added an element of diversity and color to the railroad locomotive. Other countries have less variety because they took a more unified or standardized approach toward locomotive design, acquisition, and classification.

The history of the American locomotive is illustrated by many different designs. Some were experimental, others tried and true. This book examines the different locomotive types, exploring 10 steam, 5 electric, and 15 diesel locomotive categories. The examples portrayed are worthy of attention for a variety of reasons. Some are noteworthy feats of engineering that are held in especially high regard by students of locomotive technology; others are famous engines made popular through advertising and pictures. Many are noteworthy for their distinctive appearance, or as examples of important technological advancements.

The locomotive categories illustrated have been deliberately varied to include many different eras, railroads, manufacturers, types, and models, as well as different types of service for which the locomotives were intended. Some of the entries focus on a single class of locomotive operated by just one railroad, while others cover a group of models used by many different lines. For example, the Big Boy was a specialized locomotive operated by just one railroad; the Electro-Motive F-unit encompassed more than a dozen different models, used by more than 100 different North American lines.

In the last century, hundreds of books have been written on locomotives. These include detailed manuals for operation; general histories detailing development, application, and production; and extremely focused, detailed histories that chronicle one railroad's fleet, just one specific model, and in a few cases, one specific locomotive.

This book is not a complete history or a spotter's guide; nor is it a technical manual, but rather a celebration of locomotives through great photographs, interesting histories, and relevant statistics. It aims to entertain and inform by showing photographs of locomotives in their working environment, describing the history behind them, and explaining the jobs they performed. Some of these locomotives are antique, obsolete designs that were forsaken for scrap years ago, while others are modern state-of-the-art machines that are working on American mainlines today.

Top: A good switcher seemingly lasted forever. Boston &Maine 0-6-0 No. 427 was a relatively young 21 years old when it was photographed at Northampton, Massachusetts, in 1934. This locomotive was scrapped in 1953 after 40 years of good service to the B&M. *Photo by Donald Shaw, Robert A. Buck collection*

Middle: A General Electric C30-7A rolls west across the Quaboag River at West Warren, Massachusetts. *Brian Solomon*

Bottom: Amtrak's former New Haven Railroad FL9s at Albany-Rensselaer, New York, on October 9, 1993. *Brian Solomon*

A Burlington Northern Santa Fe DASH 9-44CW in brilliant "warbonnet" dress rolls westward through New Mexico's Abo Canyon. *Brian Solomon*

THE STEAM LOCOMOTIVE

New York Central's 4-6-4 Hudson No. 5281, a J-1d, rests at the Boston & Albany yards at West Springfield, Massachusetts, on December 15, 1947. Within a decade New York Central would end steam operations and scrap most of its modern steam locomotives, including all of its famous Hudsons. *Jay Williams collection*

The American steam locomotive is a sublime and beautiful machine, fascinating to watch in motion. Its billowing smoke, escaping steam, thrusting pistons and rods, and spinning wheels tell the story of motive power. Unlike the basic mechanisms of other machines and locomotives, the steam locomotive's workings are not hidden. Its parts are out in the open and exposed for scrutiny and study. While there is no limit to the level of detail in which one can describe a steam locomotive and its workings, there is also no prerequisite knowledge for appreciating one in motion. People of all ages are captivated at the sight of a steam locomotive. It seems the most alive of any product of the industrial revolution. Young children will always be thrilled by steam locomotives, and no advance in technology can ever change that.

There are many different types of steam locomotives. They are distinguished from one another by their wheel arrangement. North American steam locomotive types are classified by the Whyte system, whereby the wheels are divided into three basic groupings and counted. These groups are the leading wheels, the driving wheels, and the trailing wheels. Each group of wheels is always included so that if there are no wheels in a category, a zero is used in that spot. The leading wheels are always the first group, and the trailing wheels are always

the last group. There can be one or more sets of driving wheels, and these are indicated in the middle. For example, an American type locomotive, which has four leading wheels, four driving wheels, and no trailing wheels, is designated as a 4-4-0, while an Atlantic type, which has four leading wheels, four driving wheels, and two trailing wheels, is designated as a 4-4-2. Locomotives such as articulateds and Duplexes, which have more than one set of drivers and running gear, count each grouping of drivers separately. The Union Pacific's Big Boy had two sets of eight driving wheels on an articulated frame, and it's designated a 4-8-8-4. Pennsylvania's T1 Duplex had two sets of four driving wheels on a rigid frame and is known as a 4-4-4-4. (After the close of the steam era, some locomotive authorities attempted to introduce an appended classification system that used "+" symbols to indicate articulated locomotives. While the system had an undeniable logic to it, it came long after all the locomotives had been categorized and never caught on.) Locomotives without tenders, such as Forneys, that have built-in tanks are designated with a "T" following the wheel counts. A typical Forney type would be designated 0-4-4T.

In addition to the Whyte classification, most standard wheel arrangements have names. Early names were descriptive, such as the "Ten-Wheeler." Later names often represented the railroad that first

used the wheel arrangement—an example being the 2-10-2 "Santa Fe" type, which was first used by the Santa Fe Railway. This can be confusing at times because other railroads took on locomotives of this type. Thus, not all 2-10-2 or Santa Fe-type locomotives were owned or operated by the Santa Fe Railway itself.

Each individual railroad subdivided its locomotive types by class and further by subclass. The defining elements from one class to another varied from line to line, as did the classification nomenclature. One railroad might give each wheel arrangement type a letter designation. Locomotives of each wheel arrangement would be grouped with common qualities and given a letter and number designation, such as class A1, A2, etc. Further divisions indicating subtle differences in the model of an engine might be indicated by a letter suffix, thus A1a, A1b. Some railroads used logical ways of assigning their classification terminology. For example, Southern Pacific usually used the first letter of the common name of the type. Its Pacifics were Class P, and Atlantics were Class A, and so on.

The classification systems varied greatly from railroad to railroad. It is important to understand that different railroads used the same letter combinations to describe entirely different engine types. New York Central's J-3a was a 4-6-4 Hudson built by Alco, while

Chesapeake & Ohio's J-3a was a 4-8-4 Northern built by Lima. Other than the fact that both were steam locomotives on American railroads, these types had nothing in common, and their common classification is coincidental.

In this book, to vary the coverage of the text, each locomotive profile has a different level of focus. Some profiles discuss just a single class of locomotive owned by only one railroad. Others may discuss all the locomotives of a specific wheel arrangement in more general terms. For example, the Chicago & North Western R-1 is a specific class of locomotive to the C&NW. The Nickel Plate Road Berkshire is a wheel arrangement that covered three different classes of locomotive, while the 4-4-0 American type is a wheel arrangement that was built to many different specifications by dozens of different builders, for more than a hundred different railroads.

Even though steam locomotives were phased out of general use in the 1940s and 1950s, a great many steam locomotives have been preserved. Some of these are now restored to service and operate at museums and tourist railways. A few are even used on mainline excursions from time to time. So some of the types of locomotives represented can still be found in occasional service, or at least represented by static displays. Maintaining a steam locomotive is a complex and costly business. As a result, some locomotives that were regularly operated on excursions a few years ago may not be operating today. Some of the photographs illustrating the text may be relatively recent views of historic locomotives, but while the pictures may be contemporary, the technology is not. The last new steam locomotive built for a railroad company in the United States (as opposed to a replica built for a museum) was completed in 1953. Most are much older.

◀ The R-1 could be found everywhere during the steam era, working a variety of jobs on the Chicago & North Western. By December 1954, when William D. Middleton photographed several R-1s at the roundhouse in Madison, Wisconsin, these workhorses were showing their age after nearly five decades of heavy service. *William D. Middleton*

▼ The drama of a steam locomotive is most apparent on cold days when escaping steam condenses quickly, creating spectacular effects. Chicago & North Western 1385 fills the morning air with steam and smoke as its crew prepares for the run from North Freedom, Wisconsin, to Quartzite Lake. This locomotive was a star performer at the Mid-Continent Museum's annual Snow Train event. *Brian Solomon*

THE AMERICAN STANDARD

The American Standard type was by far the most common locomotive of the nineteenth century. Although some survived in regular service until the 1960s, the American Standard's most colorful era was in the mid-1800s, when locomotives were treated as works of art. Eureka & Palisade's Eureka, photographed at Durango, Colorado, on August 23, 2000, is a 3-foot-gauge 4-4-0 now owned privately and only occasionally operated.
John Gruber

THE AMERICAN STANDARD

No locomotive has better captured the public's imagination than the American Standard. This locomotive typified the American railroad of the nineteenth century and remains the most readily identified of all steam locomotives. It was the most widely built type, and one of the longest lived. The 4-4-0 wheel arrangement with a pivoting lead bogie-truck defines the type, which is also called just an "American" or an "Eight-Wheeler."

Some of the most famous North American locomotives were examples of the American standard. Western & Atlantic's *General* was a renowned Civil War-era locomotive, commandeered by Union raiders and chased for miles by pursuing Confederate troops. Another two Americans, Central Pacific's *Jupiter* and Union Pacific's No. 119, are perhaps the most famous locomotives of all time. On May 10, 1869, at Promontory, Utah, it was these two Americans that met, in the words of Bret Harte, "Pilots touching, head to head, facing on the single track, half a world behind each back." The pictures of the completion of the Transcontinental Railroad have been reproduced thousands of times, and nearly everyone has seen images of these locomotives at one time or another.

While the colorful, ornately decorated Victorian machine is the type best remembered and most often pictured, less colorful 4-4-0s had their day in the sun, too. Twenty-four years to the day after the celebrations at Promontory, another American-type would make news. The New York Central & Hudson River Railroad built a specially designed 4-4-0 with enormous 7-foot driving wheels to haul its *Empire State Express*, known as the "fastest train in the world." On May 10, 1893, this locomotive, number 999, staged a publicity run west of Rochester, New York, where it reportedly hit an astounding speed of 112.5 miles per hour! While many authorities doubt the validity of this achievement, at the time No. 999 was world famous. Today the celebrated engine, albeit with smaller driving wheels, is preserved at the Chicago Museum of Science.

In their formative years, American railroads used a potpourri of locomotive designs, some derived from British practice, others home grown. Early imported British locomotives proved inadequate for lightly built American tracks. In Britain, a greater level of investment permitted a better track standard than prevailed in the United States. As a result, early British locomotive designs did not perform well on this side of the Atlantic Ocean and had a tendency to chew up the track and derail. To correct for this, hybrid locomotives were developed that featured a pilot and guide wheels. This improved a locomotive's tracking ability, minimizing the chance of derailment because of uneven track or because of collision with animals on the right-of-way. One of the most successful and popular early designs was the 4-2-0, which featured a two-axle leading bogie truck, introduced in 1832 by American railroad pioneer John B. Jervis. While this type was widely used in the 1830s and 1840s, its single pair of drivers did not provide enough traction, so bigger types were developed.

The first 4-4-0 was created by Henry R. Campbell, the chief engineer of the Philadelphia, Germantown & Norristown Railway, who patented the type in 1836. This wheel arrangement was improved a year later with flexible running gear, which gave the locomotive a three-point suspension system. The three-point suspension, and pair of driving wheels per side, gave the 4-4-0 the winning combination that would make it the most popular type of the nineteenth century. It was flexible,

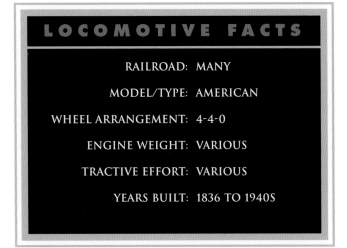

LOCOMOTIVE FACTS

RAILROAD: MANY

MODEL/TYPE: AMERICAN

WHEEL ARRANGEMENT: 4-4-0

ENGINE WEIGHT: VARIOUS

TRACTIVE EFFORT: VARIOUS

YEARS BUILT: 1836 TO 1940S

versatile, and powerful, making it the ideal engine for most situations. Still, it took a decade for the American type to come into vogue, and yet another decade after that for it to achieve its familiar form.

The first 4-4-0s shared primitive characteristics with other early types. By the mid-1850s, 4-4-0s were being built with cabs to protect the engine crew, and they used improved components, such as Stephenson valve gear and the wagon top boiler—both of which came to typify locomotive construction in the second half of the nineteenth century. Many locomotives of the period were built as wood burners, requiring elaborate smokestacks to prevent burning embers from escaping and starting wildfires. One of the most common types of stack was the large, conical "balloon" stack. In the last quarter of the nineteenth century, most railroads switched from wood fuel to coal. This change precipitated the end of the colorful, highly polished, elaborately decorated locomotive. By the mid-1880s, many locomotives were wearing a utilitarian "basic black," reflecting the sooty, dirty nature of coal. The need for elaborate smokestacks was also diminished. The 4-4-0 wheel arrangement survived, but its appearance was more subdued in later years.

While all American types, by definition, shared a common wheel arrangement, the size and power of the locomotives varied greatly. The earliest 4-4-0s weighed just 12 to 15 tons. Later versions weighed as much as 45 tons. Many 4-4-0s were built to the standard 4-foot, 8.5-inch track gauge, though some Americans were built to 6-foot gauge for the broad-gauge Erie Railroad. Scaled-down versions were built to smaller sizes for narrow-gauge lines.

Other developments, such as knuckle couplers, automatic air brakes, and more advanced signaling systems, facilitated the operation of much longer and heavier trains. As trains grew heavier, new and more powerful locomotives were developed, superseding the dominance of the 4-4-0. By the late 1880s, the 4-4-0 was already in decline.

It was still being used in large numbers, but it was no longer preferred for heavy freight assignments. At the turn of the century, roughly 11,000 American types were still owned by North American railways. As railways continued to purchase bigger and more powerful locomotives, the 4-4-0 was relegated to secondary duties on branch lines and other places where bigger locomotives were unsuitable. The last American 4-4-0s were built in the 1940s for export to Mexico. Some survived in daily revenue service on the Canadian Pacific until the early 1960s.

BOSTON & MAINE CLASS B-15 MOGUL

Boston & Maine 2-6-0 No. 1401 steams in the winter sun in Somerville, Massachusetts, on February 28, 1934.
Steam locomotives were everywhere in 1934, and the sight of a simmering Mogul was no more unusual at
that time than a 737 flying overhead today. **Photo by Donald Shaw, Robert A. Buck collection**

On January 17, 1956, Boston & Maine Mogul No. 1455 rolls westbound through Weston, Massachusetts, during a heavy snowfall. A few months after this photograph was made, the B&M would end steam operations. This locomotive was one of the lucky ones. It was purchased by the late Nelson Blount and is preserved today in Connecticut. *H. Bentley Crouch*

BOSTON & MAINE CLASS B-15 MOGUL

The 2-6-0 wheel arrangement was introduced around 1860 as a powerful freight locomotive that placed most of its weight on drivers for greater adhesion. Compared to the tiny, antique-looking 4-4-0 American Standard locomotives of the period, the 2-6-0 seemed rather large, so the type was labeled the "Mogul" to convey its size and greater power—a mogul being an emperor or powerful businessman. While the Mogul type never became as popular as the 4-4-0 or 4-6-0, it was built in large numbers during the second half of the nineteenth century. Alfred Bruce, author of *The Steam Locomotive in America*, estimates that 8,000 Moguls were built for domestic service between 1860 and 1910.

The Boston & Maine inherited a number of older Mogul types from predecessor lines, particularly the Fitchburg Railroad, but the B&M is best remembered for its Class B-15s, built between 1903 and 1910. The handed-down Moguls resembled machines from the earlier period, while the B-15s exhibited a more modern appearance representative of early twentieth century locomotives. It may seem strange to describe something as old as a Mogul as looking modern, but in steam locomotive terms, they were modern for the time. The B-15s were well-proportioned, utilitarian machines with fairly large boilers, straight smokestacks, rounded steam and sand domes, and steel pilots.

Boston & Maine's B-15s were unusual because by 1903 the 2-6-0 wheel arrangement had largely fallen out of favor. The 2-8-0s were preferred for heavy freight work, and the 2-8-2 Mikado had just been introduced. Passenger types were getting ever larger and faster. While many lines still used big 4-4-0s, a number of new types were on the scene, including 2-6-2s, 4-4-2s, and the fabled 4-6-2 Pacific. Yet B&M made excellent use of its late-era 2-6-0s, which featured relatively tall (63-inch) driving wheels and 19x26-inch cylinders. The locomotives were lightweight, powerful, and versatile machines that were well suited for a variety of duties. They worked branch line freights, mixed trains, milk runs, suburban passenger trains, and yard jobs. They were especially well suited to hauling short passenger trains of four or five wooden cars.

They were good on snow jobs too—it's no joke. New England winters can be notoriously tough, and drifting snow slows operations and demands special equipment. B&M had a significant fleet of wedge snowplows, but in the winter it also fitted some of its B-15s with large pilot plows to accommodate blowing, drifting snow.

B&M's 137 B-15s were all built by Alco, some at its Schenectady Locomotive Works. Most, however, were built at Alco's Manchester Locomotive Works in New Hampshire, a facility that built many locomotives over the years for Boston & Maine and its predecessor lines. Years later, B&M rebuilt some of the B-15s with superheaters to improve their thermal efficiency. Superheated steam was much hotter than saturated steam, and hotter steam required a more advanced valve design. So B&M fitted the rebuilt B-15s with Franklin economy steam chests—tall boxy valve assemblies that sat atop the cylinders. During rebuilding, the Moguls were also fitted with modern steel cabs to replace the conventional wooden cabs they had when they were delivered.

Boston & Maine's Moguls are remembered because of their longevity. They survived in revenue service longer than many other types. A few remained in service until 1956, putting them among the last steam locomotives to operate in regular service in New England. Boston & Maine was quick to adopt diesels for mainline freight services, and in the early 1940s, it ordered a large fleet of Electro-Motive FTs, followed by subsequent F-unit types. As a result of these new diesels, B&M's largest and heaviest steam power was made surplus fairly early, and a decade before the last of the Moguls were retired, much newer power was purged from the roster. By the mid-1950s, B&M had retired, sold, or scrapped most of its later or larger types. Its big 2-10-2 Santa Fe types, Class S-1, built 10 years after the B-15s, were gone by 1950. Some of its powerful 2-8-4 Berkshires, built by Lima in 1928 and 1929, were sold to Southern Pacific and Santa Fe during World War II, and the remainder scrapped after the war. B&M's 18 late-era 4-8-2 Mountains, built by Baldwin between 1935 and 1941, had relatively short careers in New England. In 1947, B&M sold most of these to the Baltimore & Ohio, where they toiled away in coal service for a few more years.

So while the memory of more modern locomotives was fading, the veteran Moguls still soldiered on in daily service. They were to be found all over the railroad, but in their last years the Moguls were primarily assigned to Boston suburban passenger trains on the Saugus Branch and the old Central Mass route that ran due west from Boston to Northampton. In suburban service they were a true anachronism, hauling a ragtag "splinter fleet"—wooden passenger cars that survived long after most trains had been converted to steel equipment. These wooden cars survived because they did not work in interstate service. If they still ran today, these quaint "modern" Moguls hauling short trains of wooden cars would be a major tourist attraction. No doubt they would be heralded in the same fashion as San Francisco's famous cable cars, and New Orleans' conventional electric streetcars. Tourist lines all across the country strive to recreate the era of small steam locomotives and traditional passenger cars, and generally they do so with less success, and certainly less authenticity, than what the B&M was running daily in the mid-1950s. Yet in the 1950s, hardly anyone thought the Moguls were an attraction. They were seen as antique and dirty, to be tolerated at best, but certainly not admired! "Oh no, not those old things, and the cars they haul, what pitiful relics they are."

In 1956 they made their final runs, and were replaced unceremoniously with a fleet of sleek, modern Budd-built rail diesel cars (RDCs). The daily commuter must have cheered a mighty "haroo" with this perceived improvement. The RDCs were clean, air-conditioned, and modern in every way. For more than three decades to follow, the RDC was the staple of the Boston area suburban passenger service. When they too were finally retired in the early 1990s, no doubt they suffered the same complaints and scorn endured by the unfortunate Moguls.

While Boston suburban service has thrived in recent years, the old Central Mass line, still remembered for the old Moguls, has fallen into disuse. The tracks are a weed-covered memory of an earlier era. The final RDC trip over the line was run in the 1970s, and freight service ended about 1980. Depots along the line lay derelict, and the crossings with local highways have been removed. But on a still, wintry night, you can find your way to the tracks, empty these many years, and imagine a B-15 sprinting toward North Station, smoke and steam pouring from its stack, as its whistle echoes through the towns and villages along the line.

Not all of B&M's B-15s were scrapped. One locomotive, No. 1455, was sold to the late Nelson Blount in 1956. For many years it was displayed at Edaville, a tourist railway at South Carver, Massachusetts. Recently the locomotive was moved, and it is now at a museum in Connecticut. It is one of only a handful of B&M steam locomotives to escape scrapping.

On March 6, 1954, Boston & Maine Mogul 1496 leads passenger train No. 3104 eastward over the Central Mass line near Berlin, Massachusetts. This Mogul was fitted with a large plow. *Photo by Stan K. Bolton, Jr., courtesy George C. Corey*

LOCOMOTIVE FACTS

RAILROAD: BOSTON & MAINE

MODEL/TYPE: B-15B, MOGUL

WHEEL ARRANGEMENT: 2-6-0

ENGINE WEIGHT: 138,250 LBS.

TRACTIVE EFFORT: 25,300 LBS.

YEARS BUILT: 1903-1910

FORNEY TANK

Sandy River & Rangeley Lakes No. 22 was typical of the Maine 2-foot-gauge Forneys. Although this locomotive was scrapped, SR&RL No. 5 was preserved through the efforts of Frank Ramsdell and his daughter Alice, who maintained the locomotive on a private estate. **Photo by Donald Shaw, Robert A. Buck collection**

S.R.&R.L   22

▲ This locomotive was used by the 6th Avenue elevated line in Manhattan, a popular stomping ground for Forneys in the late nineteenth and early twentieth centuries. These lightweight locomotives had relatively high tractive effort and were ideal for negotiating the sharp curves and steel inclines associated with the elevated lines of New York and Chicago. *Richard Jay Solomon collection*

▶ An artist's rendition of New York Elevated Railroad No. 39, a typical Forney type used on the New York elevated lines. The elevated railways were rapid transit lines designed to move large volumes of passengers over city streets on large iron causeways. The Forneys were eventually displaced when the "Els" were electrified. *Richard Jay Solomon collection*

FORNEY TANK

The advent of heavy suburban passenger traffic placed new demands on American railroads. Suburban passengers had different requirements from those using conventional trains, and railroads found that to accommodate suburban traffic they needed to run short, frequent trains on regular intervals. These trains carried the bulk of their passengers in one direction in the morning, and the other direction in the evening. Suburban trains had relatively short runs, but needed to make frequent stops and maintain tight schedules. Also, to obtain maximum utilization of equipment, trains needed to be able to reverse directions at terminals quickly. These conditions led to the design of a specialized locomotive called a "tank engine."

Conventional steam locomotives carried coal and water in a tender—a separate car that trailed behind the engine and was semi-permanently coupled to it. Instead of a traditional tender, the tank locomotive carried its coal and water on the engine. This made for a much shorter locomotive, and made reverse moves easier because the locomotive did not have to push the tender when running backward—reducing the risk of derailment and making it easier for the engineer to see where he was headed. Another advantage of the tank design was that it placed the full weight of the locomotive and its fuel on the drivers, which provided greater adhesion. Yet there were a couple of disadvantages to the tank arrangements that precluded their adoption in general service. They could only carry a relatively small amount of fuel and water, which greatly restricted their range between service stops. More importantly, as their fuel was depleted, it lessened the weight of the locomotive and reduced its adhesion, giv-

ing less and less pulling power as it rolled along. Although the locomotives could easily operate in reverse, railroads found this resulted in increased rail wear, as a result of the lack of rear guide wheels and the greater weight of the firebox end of the locomotive.

Some of the earliest tank locomotives were built as switchers, where a short locomotive was desirable and the limitations of short range and variable adhesion were of minimal concern. Later the tank locomotive was developed into a suburban passenger locomotive, a task for which it was nearly ideally suited. Suburban passenger trains only required a short-range locomotive, and needed a high adhesion machine for rapid acceleration, without the need for great speed. Since tank engines could operate in either direction, this simplified turning procedures and meant the locomotive could simply run around its train at the end of the run and did not need to be rotated on a turntable.

In the 1870s, Matthias N. Forney designed a tank engine that solved some the flaws associated with older tank designs. Forney was one of America's best-known railway engineers, and was one of a few people in the industry who stepped back and forth between

EIGHT-WHEELED LOCOMOTIVE USED ON THE NEW YORK ELEVATED RAILROAD.

journalism and engineering, with successes in both fields. For many years Forney was editor and part owner of the *Railway Gazette*, one of the best known railway trade publications of the time. Later he published and edited the *Railroad and Engineering Journal*. Today he is still known for his authoritative book on locomotive practice called the *Catechism of the Locomotive*, which was a standard text in the field for many years.

Forney learned the locomotive business from Ross Winans, one of the most original locomotive builders in the United States. Unlike the vast majority of American builders, who advanced and adapted locomotives based on British practices, Winans locomotives were largely based on purely American designs.

The Forney Tank used a 0-4-4T wheel arrangement, and included a fixed tender built on an extended frame with the engine. In the *Catechism of the Locomotive*, Forney describes the benefits of his design:

In order to get all the advantages which a four-wheel switching engine possesses in having its whole weight on the driving-wheels, and at the same time avoid the disadvantages which result from a short wheelbase, and also from a varying amount of weight on the driving-wheels, [the] locomotive designed by the writer with the whole weight of the boiler and machinery resting on the driving-wheels, and the water and fuel on a truck. By this means not only the objections to carrying the weight of the water on the driving-wheels is overcome, but at the same time the disadvantages arising from the short wheel-base . . . are also obviated. That is, all the permanent weight of the boiler and machinery of such a locomotive rests on the driving-wheels, and is therefore all adhesive weight, as it is in the switching engine, and at the same time by extending the frame beyond the fire-box and placing the water-tank and fuel on this extension of the frame and supporting their weight on a truck, the engine has a wheel-base that is as long and flexible as that of ordinary American engines.

He continues his explanation,

If an ordinary American locomotive runs backward, that is with the driving-wheels in front, the friction of their flanges against the rails on curves of short radius will be very excessive. To avoid this with locomotives last described, they are run with the truck first, which, being at the opposite end of the boiler from the position that it usually occupies, reverses the position of the boiler and other parts relative to the motion of the engine. That is, the fire-box is then in front and the smoke-stack behind.

Forney's first big success with his tank engine was in the developing field of rapid transit. To better serve their growing urban populations, new elevated railways were built in New York and Chicago. Forney was a vocal proponent of urban steam-powered trains, and many of his locomotives were built for passenger service on the "Els," as the elevateds were known. While these small, relatively lightweight, yet

A Forney with its crew, circa 1900. While the spirit of the scene is captured here in black and white on an old-style glass plate negative, imagine this as it really was, in full living color. When the photographer finished, the engineer (standing on the left) asks, "Are ya done?" Then he and his fireman climb aboard the engine, sound the whistle, ring the bell, and crack the throttle. *William Bullard Archive, courtesy Dennis Lebeau*

powerful, locomotives were nearly ideally suited to elevated operations, their tenure on them was relatively short. Electrification proved to be a much better option, and shortly after the end of the nineteenth century, most of these "Forneys" had been sold or scrapped. Some former elevated Forneys found work on logging railroads, where their short flexible wheelbase, light axle loadings, high adhesion, and bidirectional ability were especially valuable. Forney also sold a number of his tank engines to railroads for suburban services, and his locomotives were often used on urban branch lines where short frequent trains were necessary.

Forney was known for his strong opinions about railway practices. One of his obsessions was deriding and decrying the advent of narrow gauge railways, one of the most popular new types of railroading in the 1870s and 1880s. This is ironic, because one of the longest lasting applications for his 0-4-4T design was on the 2-foot gauge lines in Maine. Here a number of Forneys operated in regular service until the eve of World War II. Several of these locomotives were preserved and are still in operating condition today.

Forney's promotion of tank engine design led to some confusion, and some people began referring to many tank engine designs as Forneys, whether or not they used the 0-4-4T wheel arrangement with fixed tender.

CHICAGO & NORTH WESTERN R-1

Chicago & North Western No. 1385 is disguised as Lackawanna Ten-Wheeler No. 1061 for the filming of a Steamtown promotional film. While the Lackawanna never owned a Ten-Wheeler numbered 1061, it did have several Alco-built 4-6-0s in that number series, all of which were originally camelbacks. Some were later rebuilt with single cabs.
Brian Solomon

▲ Old Chicago & North Western No. 894 is switching out a New York Central boxcar, as a man on the ground flags a highway crossing at Baraboo, Wisconsin, in December 1955. This R-1 has been rebuilt with modern piston valves (the cylindrical appendage above the driving cylinders) and Walschaerts outside valve gear. *John Gruber*

▶ On February 17, 1996, C&NW No. 1385 pulls up to the water tank at North Freedom, Wisconsin. This contemporary scene is reminiscent of a common event of an earlier generation. Built by Alco-Schenectady in 1907, locomotive 1385 was sold by C&NW in 1961 to a group of preservationists; it was later restored to service on the Mid-Continent Railway Museum. *Brian Solomon*

Chicago & North Western R-1

If any one locomotive could be selected to represent Chicago & North Western's steam power fleet, it would have to be the Class R-1 Ten-Wheeler. In its day, the R-1 was the most common, and perhaps the most versatile, locomotive on the railroad. A total of 325 R-1s were built, the most numerous type of any C&NW steam locomotive, and they were among the longest lived classes on the railroad.

The 4-6-0 Ten-Wheeler was developed prior to 1850 and initially used primarily as a heavy freight locomotive. The type was essentially an expansion of the successful 4-4-0 American (see page 12), and shared the same three-point suspension system that made the American type so well suited to American railways' lightly built track structure. The 4-6-0 grew to be the second-most popular type in the nineteenth century, and was ultimately one of the longest lived and one of the most numerous wheel arrangements ever built in North America. Locomotive historian Alfred Bruce, in his book, *The Steam Locomotive in America*, estimated more than 17,000 4-6-0s were built. Despite the advent of bigger and more powerful designs, the 4-6-0 remained in continuous production from its inception until 1920, and was built by a few lines, such as the Pennsylvania Railroad, until the mid-1930s.

Although the 4-6-0 wheel arrangement was originally conceived for heavy freight, many later 4-6-0s were built as dual-service locomotives, and around the turn of the century, some railroads adapted the type to fast passenger service by building them with large fireboxes and tall drivers. New York Central and its subsidiaries had particularly good luck with fast Ten-Wheelers, although these locomotives had a fairly short tenure on premier assignments because they were bumped by newer, more powerful engines.

Chicago & North Western did not adopt the 4-6-0 on a large scale until the mid-1880s, and relied primarily on 4-4-0 Americans, and 2-6-0 Moguls to haul the majority of its trains. Then during the last 15 years of the nineteenth century, C&NW amassed quite a variety of 4-6-0s. Most were products of the Schenectady Locomotive Works, in Schenectady, New York, but some were built by Baldwin. During that time, compound steam locomotives were a popular way of achieving greater efficiency and better fuel consumption, and C&NW experimented with compound 4-6-0 types. (A compound steam locomotive uses two sets of cylinders, one high pressure, the other low pressure, to gain thermal efficiency by using the steam twice. The high-pressure cylinders exhaust steam into the low-pressure cylinders.) C&NW tried Baldwin's Vauclain compound arrangement, which used four cylinders, and some two-cylinder cross-compound designs. C&NW even rebuilt some simple 4-6-0s into compounds, before concluding—as did most American railroads—that the advantages of compounding were outweighed by the increased maintenance costs.

Between 1897 and 1900, C&NW bought 140 Class R Ten-Wheelers, splitting the order between Schenectady and Baldwin. These locomotives had 63-inch drivers, 20x26-inch cylinders, and weighed a total of 153,000 pounds, producing 26,700 pounds tractive effort. Following the Rs were the Class R-1s, which were built between 1901 and 1908, and again the order was split between Schenectady (by this time part of the American Locomotive Company–Alco) and Baldwin. While today the R-1s seem small and quaint in comparison to more modern steam locomotives, they were considered big locomotives when they were new. To accommodate their greater weight, C&NW had to shore up many older bridges. As

originally constructed, the R-1s weighed 164,000 pounds, 7.5 tons more than the Class Rs. The R-1s were later rebuilt with larger boilers, adding a few tons of steel and bringing them up to 167,500 pounds. Most R-1s were built with traditional Stephenson valve gear, which was located between the locomotive drivers. However some later R-1s used Walschearts outside valve gear, which had come into vogue in North America after 1904.

Until the early twentieth century, C&NW applied an unorthodox way of assigning locomotive numbers, which resulted in a seemingly random numbering sequence for most of its classes. While most lines reserved sequential number blocks for locomotives of the same class and wheel arrangement, C&NW simply assigned a new locomotive the number of a recently retired locomotive. As a result, locomotives of a single class were rarely numbered in sequence, nor did they even enjoy a similar numbering pattern. The earliest R-1s were numbered in this way, while later R-1s were given small number blocks, which at least gave them some numbering continuity. Also, C&NW did not assign locomotives of one wheel arrangement a single letter class. So while the later Ten-Wheelers were Rs and R-1s, earlier 4-6-0s were given classes of D, E, Q, and S with various subclasses, sometimes intermingled with other wheel arrangements.

Because of its versatility, the R-1 worked a great variety of trains all across C&NW's far-flung Midwestern system. They could be found hauling suburban passenger trains out of North Western Terminal in Chicago, working mixed freight in Michigan's Upper Peninsula, pulling a high plains local across the wind-swept wheat fields of South Dakota, or toiling with an Iowa branch line passenger train. Many R-1s survived into the diesel era, some of them providing the railroad with five decades of service. C&NW was one of the last Midwestern lines to operate steam, finally ending steam operations in 1956.

Three R-1s escaped scrapping. One is preserved at the Forney Transportation Museum in Colorado, and another is privately owned and stored in Upper Michigan. But the best known of the three resides at the Mid-Continent Railway Museum at North Freedom, Wisconsin. C&NW R-1, No. 1385, was acquired by Mid-Continent members for $2,600 in 1961. It was restored to service in 1963, and used to haul the museum's first passenger train on a short former C&NW branch line. For six years between 1964 and 1970, the locomotive was out of service. Over the next three decades it became a popular tourist attraction, visited by tens of thousands of railroad enthusiasts over the years. Thanks to the dedication of Mid-Continent volunteers and the help of C&NW employees during the mid-1980s, 1385 locomotive hauled numerous excursions along the lines operated by its original owner. It also made mainline trips on Wisconsin Central, and Wisconsin & Southern lines in central Wisconsin.

In the later 1990s, 1385 was relegated to operation on Mid-Continent's home rails, where it was often the star attraction of the museum's Snow Train excursions, held in February. This is one of the few steam events in North America held during the winter, as the majority of steam excursions and museums only operate during the spring and summer. During its nearly 40-year excursion career, 1385 became one of the most popular and most photographed steam locomotives in the Midwest. It has been featured in numerous magazines and books, and was even disguised as a Delaware, Lackawanna & Western 4-6-0 for the filming of a Steamtown promotional film. (Steamtown is located in Scranton, Pennsylvania, at the site of Lackawanna's shops. It runs over a short portion of Lackawanna mainline, but doesn't have any operating Lackawanna steam locomotives.) As of this writing, C&NW 1385 is awaiting restoration at North Freedom.

C&NW No. 1385 leads an excursion up grade, out of the yard at North Freedom, Wisconsin. The R-1 was built to operate with 200 pounds boiler pressure. It had 30,900 pounds tractive effort as built, although many locomotives were later rebuilt, altering their weight and tractive effort slightly. *Brian Solomon*

THE 0-6-0 SWITCHER

An 0-6-0 switching was once a common sight all across North America. Today, the Conway Scenic Railroad proudly operates a former Grand Trunk Railway 0-6-0 on its historic passenger trains out of North Conway, New Hampshire. Prior to its excursion career, this locomotive spent most of its life working for the Canadian National.
Brian Solomon

flexible, lightweight nature of the track structure demanded locomotives with guiding wheels and good suspension.

In the 1870s, there was renewed interest in the 0-6-0 type, when this wheel arrangement was applied to compact heavy switching locomotives. A switcher is normally assigned slow-speed drilling tasks, where it is required to haul heavy tonnage over short distances. It needs high tractive effort, but doesn't need to operate at great speed or over long distances. In the steam era, the 0-6-0 ideally fulfilled these requirements. It allowed for a light engine with good adhesion, equipped with relatively small wheels for high tractive effort, and with a short wheelbase that allowed it to easily negotiate sharp curves at slow speeds. Thus an 0-6-0 switcher could work in a variety of different places where road locomotives were ill-suited or prohibited because of size or weight. The 0-6-0 could easily weave through complicated track layouts with a long string of loaded coal hoppers in tow, move a 10-car passenger train from a coach yard to the terminal, spot boxcars on tight industrial trackage, or deliver tank cars along the

THE 0-6-0 SWITCHER

The 0-6-0 wasn't known for its stellar achievements, high performance characteristics, or aesthetic attributes. It was simply a ubiquitous workhorse locomotive that toiled in the shadows, making up trains for the larger, higher profile machines. The 0-6-0 type was designed and built for lowly switching services, and rarely received recognition from locomotive authorities, publicists, or storytellers. Yet despite its low profile, this unsung hero served an essential role for railroads across the nation and elsewhere. It gathered cars and made up trains hauled by bigger, faster, and more impressive locomotives that are much better known.

The 0-6-0 wheel arrangement was among the earliest types built for high adhesion service, and like other early locomotive arrangements, the 0-6-0 originated in England. In the formative years of railroad development, 0-6-0 models were occasionally used for road freight service in the United States, but the arrangement quickly fell out of favor when more advanced locomotives, with guiding wheels, were designed. While the 0–6–0 had the advantage of placing its full weight on its drivers, it suffered from poor tracking ability. Thus it was undesirable for mainline service on North American lines, where the

▲ Boston & Maine No. 723, a Class G-10 switcher with 19x24-inch cylinders, was built by the Manchester Locomotive Works in 1905. It is nearly new in this photograph, taken at Worcester, Massachusetts, by William Bullard, a Worcester-based professional photographer with a personal interest in trains. *William Bullard Archive, courtesy Dennis Lebeau*

▸ The entire New Haven Railroad has been described as one big railway terminal. Its lines blanketed Connecticut, Rhode Island, and southeastern Massachusetts, serving numerous factories, warehouses, and industrial sites. On March 23, 1936, New Haven 0-6-0 Class T-1-b pauses at East Hartford, Connecticut. *Photo by Donald Shaw, Robert A. Buck collection*

docks. They were capable of climbing short steep grades, working curving industrial trackage, and meandering through rarely used street trackage.

An 0-6-0's simple, light construction meant it was comparatively inexpensive, making it popular with the railroads, which didn't wish to spend any more money than they had to on switching engines. The typical 0-6-0 of the early 1870s would have weighed a little more than 26 tons, much less than the average road locomotive of the period. It would have had smaller cylinders as well, maybe just 14x22 inches. Since the switcher rarely strayed far from the yard, it did not require a very large tender to store fuel and water. The diameter of the driving wheels was a reflection of the locomotive's intended speed. A switcher's driving wheels were among the smallest of any locomotives, often measuring just 50 inches in diameter, compared to 72- to 80-inch drivers on a fast passenger locomotives, and 57-inch drivers on heavy freight engines of the period. Although they were not flashy machines, a switcher of this time would have had some adornment, perhaps some decorative ironwork to support the headlight, an ornate lip on the smokestack, and painted accents on the drive wheels.

By comparison, later 0-6-0s were heavier, utilitarian machines that reflected the increased weight of railroad cars, and the general trend toward a uniform, uncluttered appearance that embodied the American railroad locomotive aesthetic at the turn of the century. By 1900, there were roughly 4,000 0-6-0 switchers working in the United States. An 0-6-0 of period would have weighed 55 tons and had 18x24-inch cylinders, and yet would have retained the same basic plan as the early machines. Its drive wheels would still have been only 50 to 52 inches in diameter. Since switchers were rarely afforded the extra expense of state-of-the-art technology, and many railroads didn't wish to invest in the cost of updating their switching designs, improvements such as compounding and superheating were not immediately applied to most 0-6-0 types. Many lines just ordered switchers to the same plans year after year, with only the most minor modifications. There were exceptions, however, and a few lines, such as the Boston & Albany, experimented with switchers that used modern cross-compound designs. In later years, when compounding fell out of favor, switchers were built with superheaters.

After the end of the nineteenth century, the 0-6-0 type was designed to much larger proportions, and as might be expected they were heavier and more powerful. This was necessitated by the growth of American railroad cars and the gradual switch from all-wooden to all-steel car construction. The first all-steel passenger cars dated to 1907, but by the mid-1920s, most passenger trains used all-steel consists. This resulted in much heavier trains, and the switchers needed to keep pace with the road locomotives in their ability to move the cars effectively. A switcher of the 1910 period would have weighed 75 tons, had 20x26-inch cylinders, and delivered 32,800 pounds tractive effort.

Generally speaking, switchers had poor utilization compared to mainline locomotives—that is, a switcher was not working much of the time. While a mainline locomotive would be out sprinting along with a train, the switcher would spend a great amount of time sitting in the yard, waiting. When it did work, it would only travel a few hundred feet at slow speed. An 0-6-0 rarely would have the opportunity to travel more than 15 to 20 miles per hour.

Steam switchers were the first locomotives seriously threatened by the incursion of diesel-electric power. In the mid-1920s the first diesels were developed specifically to supplant steam switchers in New York City, as a result of strict air pollution legislation. Once the railroads had a taste of the diesel switcher, the concept spread fairly quickly. During the first two decades of commercial diesel-electric production, the diesel switcher was the most popular locomotive category. Diesels had a great advantage over steam in switching service because they developed high tractive effort at slow speeds, and required far less servicing than steam. By the end of steam production, roughly 15,000 0-6-0s had been manufactured for domestic use, making the 0-6-0 one of the most widely produced locomotives built in the United States. They remain a common type at railroad museums and on tourist lines, and 112 of them are preserved in North America. The 0-6-0 wheel arrangement is still popular for switching locomotives in Europe, although these are diesel or electrically powered.

So useful, yet so rarely photographed, the 0-6-0 switcher was a basic workhorse locomotive. This engine was the Baldwin Locomotive Works' plant switcher at Eddystone, Pennsylvania. It's fitting that the engine that helped in the construction of so many locomotives is now preserved for all to see at Steamtown in Scranton, Pennsylvania. *Brian Solomon*

NICKEL PLATE ROAD BERKSHIRE

On October 11, 1952, Nickel Plate Road No. 741 leads a westbound freight at Athol Springs, New York, about 10 miles west of Buffalo. The Berkshire type was the first superpower locomotive, built to efficiently haul more freight faster than any previous type. The success of the Berkshire led to a host of new superpower designs. George C. Corey

▲ Nickel Plate Road No. 765 was one of several of the railroad's Berkshires that were set for preservation. In 1963, it was donated to the city of Fort Wayne, Indiana, and for many years the Fort Wayne Historical Society operated No. 765 in excursion service. As of the winter of 2001, the locomotive was awaiting restoration. *Brian Solomon*

▸ The awe-inspiring power of big steam made railway enthusiasts of many boys during the heyday of railroads. A high-stepping Nickel Plate Road Berkshire, racing along at 70 miles per hour with a long train, could catch anyone's attention. Nickel Plate Road No. 765 leads an excursion train near Buffalo in 1989. *Brian Solomon*

NICKEL PLATE ROAD BERKSHIRE

The Berkshire type was developed in the mid-1920s by Lima's Will Woodard for the New York Central's Boston & Albany line. It was essentially an expansion of the already successful 2-8-2 Mikado type, and intended for moderately fast freight service in heavily graded territory. When it proved worthy of its task, the Boston & Albany ordered a fleet of 2-8-4s, and the type was appropriately named for B&A's Berkshire crossing. The 2-8-4 Berkshire's secret to success was its large firebox and boiler, which supplied ample quantities of steam, enabling the locomotive to operate at sustained speed, even when climbing a long grade.

In its first few years, the Berkshire was built with 63-inch drivers, which limited its speed potential. A few lines bought 2-8-4s in this original configuration, including B&A's neighbor, Boston & Maine, which also crossed the Berkshires. Flatland Illinois Central purchased Lima's original 2-8-4 prototype and acquired its own fleet of similarly proportioned Berkshires for its heavy freight services.

In the late 1920s, the Berkshire evolved into a new form. The Van Sweringen brothers of Cleveland, Ohio, had been assembling a network of railroads in the Midwest. Part of their empire was Midwestern bridge line Nickel Plate Road, which connected Buffalo with Chicago and St. Louis, by way of several significant cities in Ohio and Indiana, including their hometown. At the end of 1926, the Van Sweringens asked one of their top operations men, John J. Bernet, to

give up his presidency of the Nickel Plate, in order to take charge of the Erie Railroad—then one of the most recent lines to enter the Van Sweringen fold. One of Bernet's first moves was to modernize the Erie's locomotive fleet, which was then characterized by a collection of poorly maintained antiques.

Bernet was enamored with the potential of the Berkshire type and ordered a fleet of 2-8-4s from Alco. These locomotives advanced the basic Berkshire design, allowing for an even faster heavy freight locomotive by employing significantly larger drivers—70 inches instead of 63 inches. They also used precision wheel balancing techniques to minimize the destructive effects of dynamic augment (damaging reciprocation forces). Dynamic augment had limited the maximum speed of most earlier heavy freight locomotive designs. Erie's Berkshires were larger and more powerful than the earlier machines, partly attributable to Erie's broader loading gauge, an effect of Erie's broad track gauge that was used until the 1880s. (While most American lines use 4-foot, 8.5-inch track, the Erie system was built with 6-foot-wide track.) Erie's Berkshires weighed over 30 tons more than those used on the B&A. Ultimately the Erie assembled a fleet of 105 2-8-4s, the largest in the United States. Despite the success of the Alco 2-8-4s, Erie's later orders were split between Alco's competitors, Lima and Baldwin. This gave Erie the rare distinction of having examples of one type of locomotive from each of the three major builders.

The success of the Erie Berkshire led fellow-Van Sweringen road, Chesapeake & Ohio, to adapt and expand the type into a 2-10-4 Texas type (the next logical progression from a 2-8-4). Like Erie's Berkshires, these locomotives were extremely successful, and used large drivers for relatively fast freight operation. In 1933, Bernet returned to the Nickel Plate Road, and used his experience on the Erie to improve the NKP's steam locomotive fleet. By this time the Van Sweringen lines had established a joint motive power design group called the Advisory Mechanical Committee, which was in charge of procuring the best standard designs for the different railroads. Bernet encouraged the design of a 2-8-4, and the AMC came up with one that embodied many of the best features of the Erie's 2-8-4 and the C&O's 2-10-4.

Nickel Plate Road 765 marches through Black Rock in Buffalo, New York, on July 2, 1989. *Brian Solomon*

The first of these machines were built by Alco in 1934, designated Class S, and carried the numbers 700 to 714. They used slightly smaller drivers than Erie's Berkshires, 69 inches, and used a small-bore, long-stroke cylinder design combined with an ample boiler and high working pressure to produce a more compact machine with high performance potential. The first 15 Berkshires satisfied the railroad's motive power needs during the Depression, when traffic levels were relatively low.

Following the advent of World War II, Nickel Plate, like all American railroads, found itself needing more power. In 1942 and 1943, Lima built 25 Berkshires based on the design of its earlier machines. Lima followed with another 30 Berkshires in 1944. Both orders of wartime 2-8-4s were designated Class S-2 and numbered in sequence after the original Class S 2-8-4s. After the war, when most lines began

to order new diesels and were largely abandoning steam, Nickel Plate bucked the trend by placing one last order for Berkshires, 10 Class S-3s, built by Lima in 1949. Nickel Plate Road 779 had the distinction of being not only the last Lima steam locomotive built, but the last domestic 2-8-4 constructed as well.

Nickel Plate's Berkshires had a characteristic appearance that had common qualities with many AMC designs. The locomotives were noted for a solid, well-balanced design, and featured such modern attributes as an extra large sand dome with the railroad's initials painted on it in gold lettering. Twelve external sand line feeds, six on each side of the engine, radiated from the dome. A number of railroads, including fellow Van Sweringen lines Pere Marquette, Wheeling, and eventually even the C&O, bought 2-8-4s based on the Nickel Plate's. (The C&O's locomotives, however, were always known as

A detailed study of the crosshead and lead driving wheel on Nickel Plate Road No. 765. The crosshead transmits the power of the cylinders to the main rod. *Brian Solomon*

On an overcast afternoon in the spring of 1968, Nickel Plate Road No. 759 leads an excursion near Albany, New York. This locomotive thrilled thousands of people on its excursions in the late 1960s and early 1970s. Today it is preserved at Steamtown in Scranton, Pennsylvania. *Richard Jay Solomon*

▲ Lima's A1 2-8-4 proved its merit on the Boston & Albany, hauling freight east from Selkirk, New York. In 1930, New York Central's Lima-built A1b No. 1435 leads a freight out of the State Line Tunnel near Canaan, New York. *Photo by H. W. Pontin, J. R. Quinn collection*

Kanawhas, rather than Berkshires.) The Virginian, as well as the Richmond, Fredricksburg & Potomac, also bought locomotives with the same basic proportions.

Nickel Plate assigned its Berkshires to fast freights between Chicago, Cleveland, and Buffalo, and in later years strengthened its infrastructure to allow them to run on its line to St. Louis. Much of the Nickel Plate Road was built adjacent to New York Central's "Water Level Route," and in the mid-1950s NKP's Berkshires gained fame by outpacing New York Central diesels on parallel tracks. Nickel Plate was one of very few American lines that hauled "piggy back" flatcars behind steam. Intermodal transport was just catching on as railroads were disposing of their steam fleets, and the two technologies, each associated with different eras, only overlapped by a few years. Nickel Plate was among the last American lines to operate mainline freight behind steam, finally switching to diesels in the summer of 1958.

A number of Nickel Plate's handsome Berkshires were preserved, and two have become famous for their excursion work. In the late 1960s and early 1970s, NKP 759 operated a number of public excursions, and even hauled a few freight trains on Erie-Lackawanna, and Western Maryland. Today 759 is part of the Steamtown collection in Scranton, Pennsylvania. NKP 765, based in Fort Wayne, Indiana, has operated excursions in the Midwest and East, including over some of its former Nickel Plate stomping grounds. The Nickel Plate Road itself only barely survived the steam era. In 1964 the railroad lost its identity when it was bought by the Norfolk & Western. Today former Nickel Plate lines are operated by the gigantic Norfolk Southern, one of the largest railway companies in the East.

NEW YORK CENTRAL HUDSON

Without question, the New York Central Hudson was one of the finest locomotive types ever built. They were well proportioned, powerful, fast, efficient, and exceptionally reliable. New York Central J-1c No. 5401, a 1930 product of Alco-Schenectady, is seen at St. Louis, Missouri, on August 15, 1940. Jay Williams collection

NEW YORK CENTRAL HUDSON

New York Central's famous Hudsons were among the finest steam locomotives ever built. They set service and efficiency precedents that were the marvel of the industry. Though ultimately beaten by the diesel-electric, they are still fondly remembered running along their namesake river. Central's Hudsons were far more than ordinary locomotives; they were highly refined precision machines, designed to haul the railroad's long-distance passenger trains. They were the best of the best: powerful, fast, efficient, reliable, and attractive. If a New York Central Hudson ran today, thousands would come to watch it pass.

New York Central's primary artery was its famous Water Level Route, a largely four-track raceway that connected New York City and Chicago by way of Albany, Buffalo, Cleveland, and Toledo. In the golden age of the American railroad, this was one of the nation's most industrialized and heavily populated corridors, and New York Central was among the foremost American railroads—its passenger trains were world famous. The railroad's flagship, the *Twentieth Century Limited*, raced the length of the route in just over 16 hours. This all-Pullman sleeper train was *the* preferred way to travel between New York and Chicago and the pride of the company. It was fast, plush, and exclusive. To travel by the *Twentieth Century* implied importance and class. There were no coach seats on the *Century*. It was the train of diplomats, movie stars, and powerful business executives.

In the 1920s, Central was the second-largest passenger carrier in the United States. Its historical rival, the mighty Pennsylvania Railroad, was first. The prosperity of the "Roaring Twenties" gave a great boost to Central's passenger business. It needed to run longer and heavier trains to keep up with rising demand. New York Central's best Pacifics (4-6-2 wheel arrangement), its powerful K-5s, were fully capable of whisking a nine-car train at a top speed of 80 miles per hour. However, by the mid-1920s, Central found that it needed an even more powerful locomotive

to avoid costly double-heading (using two locomotives) on its long passenger trains. Central placed more severe size restrictions on locomotives than most American lines because of the tight clearances on the line, thus precluding further expansion of the successful Pacific-type. The company therefore needed to pioneer a whole new type.

New York Central's chief locomotive designer, Paul Kiefer, worked with the railroad's primary locomotive supplier, Alco, in designing a new passenger locomotive. The success of the 2-8-4 Berkshire pointed the way toward the new design. The key to sustained power is ample steam-generating capacity. More steam was more power. But more steam required a larger firebox and boiler. Thus the 4-6-2 Pacific design was expanded into a 4-6-4 to accommodate a much bigger firebox. The two-axle weight-bearing trailing truck, first applied to the Berkshire, distributed the greater weight of the expanded design, allowing the locomotive to conform to existing weight restrictions.

The Berkshire was developed for freight without aesthetic considerations. Its design was purely aimed at producing a more powerful machine. The Hudson, by contrast, was specifically intended for the railroad's premier passenger assignments, and Kiefer designed it to perform well, and look good too. Its appearance embraced a well-balanced,

utilitarian aesthetic that reflected the mechanical ideal of the period. Its headlight was centered, and extraneous equipment and plumbing was largely concealed beneath the boiler jacketing. It was not dressed up in the ornate styling of the Victorian era, nor were the original Hudsons built as streamliners—that styling would come later.

The very first 4-6-4 Hudson, New York Central No. 5200, Class J-1, debuted on Valentine's Day, 1927, roughly three years after the successful Berkshire type. It fulfilled its builder's design criteria. It was a handsome, powerful machine that featured 79-inch driving wheels, and a firebox 28 percent larger than the K-5 Pacific. Its performance was remarkably better than the K-5. The Hudson was 26 percent faster, and developed 25 percent more power. New York Central was pleased and ordered a fleet of J-1 Hudsons, which numbered 205 machines by 1931. This was a very large order for such a new machine. By comparison, New York Central's Boston & Albany had only ordered 55 of Lima's successful Berkshire design. By the early 1930s, Hudsons were handling the bulk of New York Central's intercity passenger trains. A variation of the J-1 Hudson was designed for the Boston & Albany. This was the J-2, which employed slightly smaller driving wheels, just 75 inches, to give the locomotive greater traction on the steeply graded B&A route. The order for 20 J-2s was split between Lima and Alco.

During the depths of the Depression, New York Central pushed the envelope of conventional steam locomotive design by refining its already successful Hudson. The designers applied streamlined shrouds, fine-tuned the Hudson's proportions, and incorporated modern materials.

Streamlining had become popular in the early 1930s as a way of reducing air-resistance and improving the appearance of the machines. Among the first streamlined trains were Philadelphia & Western's "Bullet Cars," Pennsylvania's famous GG1 electrics, and the new internal combustion articulated trains: Burlington's *Zephyr*, and Union Pacific's *Streamliner*. In 1934, New York Central made history as the first American railroad to apply streamlined shrouds to a steam locomotive.

Hudson 5344 was fitted with specially designed wind-resistant shrouds, inspired by Norman Zapf, a Case School of Applied Science graduate student. The locomotive was named for New York Central's consolidator, Commodore Vanderbilt. Unfortunately the shrouds interfered with locomotive maintenance, which ultimately incurred more costs than those defrayed by greater efficiency.

In 1935, New York Central debuted its J-3a "super Hudson." This design featured a host of improvements, including lightweight reciprocating parts made from modern alloyed steels, modern driving wheels instead of conventional spoked wheels, Timken tapered roller bearings, aluminum in the cabs, running boards and other equipment to reduce the weight of the engine, and shorter piston thrust. In addition, new precision wheel-balancing techniques further reduced the destructive pounding forces known as dynamic augment, which damaged both locomotives and track, and were especially severe at high speeds. The J-3s were phenomenal performers, capable of running more than 20,000 miles per month—one of the best performances ever achieved by an American steam locomotive. Ten J-3a models styled by the famous industrial designer Henry Dreyfuss were delivered as attractive streamliners. Although short-lived in service, the Dreyfuss Hudson has become a lasting symbol of the streamlined era.

In the late 1940s, new EMD E7 and Alco PA diesel-electrics assumed New York Central's premier passenger assignments, and some Hudsons were temporarily reassigned to secondary services, and even assigned to freight duties. Since they performed best moving at high speed with passenger trains, they were not well suited to hauling slower and much heavier freight trains. Sadly, none of Central's magnificent Hudsons survived the steam era. They live on only in photos, models, and memories.

New York Central J-3a No. 5344 was the first American steam locomotive treated with streamlined shrouds. This early streamlining treatment, often derided as ugly by critics, was intended to improve locomotive performance, but increased maintenance costs outweighed any savings through improved efficiency. Later Hudsons received more visually pleasing streamlining treatments.
J. R. Quinn collection

LOCOMOTIVE FACTS

RAILROAD: NEW YORK CENTRAL

MODEL/TYPE: J-3A, HUDSON

WHEEL ARRANGEMENT: 4-6-4

ENGINE WEIGHT: 360,000 LBS.

TRACTIVE EFFORT: 43,440 LBS. 12,100 LBS.
WITH BOOSTER

YEARS BUILT: 1937-1938

UNION PACIFIC BIG BOY

Although the Big Boy was not the world's largest steam locomotive—a distinction often erroneously attributed to this massive locomotive—it was nevertheless a very impressive machine. Union Pacific 4005 was photographed at Laramie, Wyoming, on November 11, 1956. Photographer unknown, Jay Williams collection

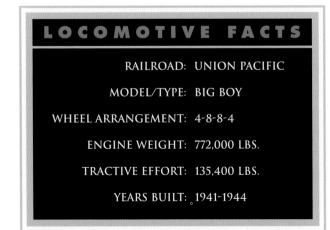

Union Pacific Big Boy No. 4007 leads a freight near Laramie, Wyoming, in August 1957. Just imagine the force of the drive rods on this powerful locomotive as they slide back and forth transmitting power to the drivers. *Richard Leonard*

UNION PACIFIC BIG BOY

Union Pacific's massive 4-8-8-4 Big Boy is considered the ultimate adaptation of the articulated steam locomotive. It was among the biggest, heaviest, and most powerful locomotives ever constructed, and certainly one of the most famous. In many respects the Big Boy represented one of the major developments in a series of evolutionary steps that began with Robert Stephenson's revolutionary *Rocket* built in 1829, a formative locomotive that influenced most subsequent development in Britain and America.

In 1904, Alco built the first large articulated locomotive for the Baltimore & Ohio. This was a 0-6-6-0 Mallet compound named *Old Maud*, designed to work as a helper on B&O's Sand Patch Grade. The Mallet type originated in Europe. It was effectively two engines under a single boiler that used two separate sets of cylinders—one high pressure and the other low pressure. In the compound arrangement, the high-pressure cylinders exhausted steam into the low-pressure cylinders, thus using the steam twice, which conserved energy and made for a more efficient locomotive. While European Mallets had been small locomotives designed for narrow gauge mountain lines, the B&O's Mallet was an enormous, standard gauge machine.

B&O's *Old Maud* was a resounding success, and within a couple of years the articulated Mallet compound had been adapted for road service. Many lines all across the United States purchased Mallets for use in heavy mainline service. The most popular wheel arrangement was the 2-6-6-2. True Mallets were easily identified by their enormous low-pressure cylinders located on the front engine, while the high-pressure

cylinders powering the rear engine were of more normal dimensions. Mallets made excellent drag freight engines. They were slow, but very powerful, and were typically assigned to long freights in graded territory. Among the most unusual Mallets were Southern Pacific's unique cab-aheads, designed for use over Donner Pass. Long snow sheds and tunnels made conventional Mallet use difficult because of the excessive smoke they emitted.

In the 1920s, Mallet compounds fell out of favor for several reasons. Among the problems were the Mallet's compound arrangement, which required considerably more maintenance than conventional "simple" locomotives. Also the heavy back pressure on the low-pressure cylinders, and small drive wheels with heavy reciprocating parts, limited the Mallet's maximum speed. By the 1920s, the slow plodding drag freight was no longer competitive with increasing highway competition, and the railroads were looking for faster freight locomotives. Although compounding was out of favor, the basic articulated locomotive design remained valid. Railroads began ordering "simple articulated" locomotives—big locomotives with two engines under one boiler, in which all cylinders were fed directly with high pressure. These locomotives were less efficient, but somewhat faster than the Mallets. They needed to have sufficient boiler capacity to feed two sets of cylinders with high-pressure steam. In the mid-1930s, further refinement allowed for the development of truly high-speed articulated locomotives.

One of the first and most successful high-speed articulated types was Union Pacific's 4-6-6-4 Challenger. This locomotive enjoyed the combined benefits of a four-wheel leading truck, tall driving wheels, and other contemporary innovations that gave it better stability at higher speeds. Unlike the early simple articulateds, which were designed to operate at a maximum of 30 to 35 miles per hour, the Challenger was designed for 70 miles per hour. It was a huge, powerful machine with great operational flexibility as a result of its articulation and power. Union Pacific assigned Challengers to both freight and passenger consists on its western mountain mainlines. A number of other railroads followed UP's lead and ordered Challengers too, making it the most successful simple articulated type.

In 1940, UP was looking for a better solution for handling heavy freights over one of its most difficult lines, the heavily graded route between Cheyenne, Wyoming, and Ogden, Utah. While not nearly as steep as some western routes, this extremely busy double-track line was difficult for UP because it required extra power to lift long trains over its grades—which was expensive and slowed operations. The two most brutal climbs were the eastbound ascent of the Wasatch Mountains just east of Odgen, and UP's legendary Sherman Hill grade, west of Cheyenne. To solve the problem, UP worked with Alco and designed a powerful 4-8-8-4 locomotive specifically suited to the task of lifting trains over the Wasatch grades. Alco had been responsible for UP's most successful recent steam designs, including its three cylinder 4-12-0s,

LOCOMOTIVE FACTS

RAILROAD: UNION PACIFIC

MODEL/TYPE: BIG BOY

WHEEL ARRANGEMENT: 4-8-8-4

ENGINE WEIGHT: 772,000 LBS.

TRACTIVE EFFORT: 135,400 LBS.

YEARS BUILT: 1941-1944

800-class 4-8-4s, and the 4-6-6-4 Challengers. The design UP and Alco came up with this time was essentially an expansion of the 4-6-6-4 Challenger type; the first and only 4-8-8-4 type ever built.

When the first 4-8-8-4 was completed, this massive machine was the world's heaviest steam locomotive. According to historian William Kratville, an Alco shop employee described the massive new type as a "Big Boy," and the name stuck. On September 4, 1941, the first Union Pacific Big Boy was delivered to Council Bluffs, Iowa. A few days later it entered service and demonstrated its might by hauling a freight train more than 100 cars long.

Traditionally big locomotives had been slow, plodding machines, and articulated locomotives in particular were known for power but not speed. The Challenger had changed this, and like the Challenger, the Big Boy was designed for both power and speed. Two Big Boys had a combined tractive effort of more than 270,000 pounds, which ought to have been enough power to move just about any train on the Union Pacific. The Big Boy could easily reach 70 miles per hour, but produced its maximum output at 30 miles per hour. Although the Big Boy is a very long locomotive (more than 132 feet), it could accommodate curves easily, and was intended to operate on curvature as tight as 20 degrees. Its size was restrictive in other ways, however, and because of these restrictions the Big Boys spent most of their careers working on the UP mainline between Cheyenne and Ogden, in the service for which they were intended. They rarely strayed from this territory because they were simply too large to fit on turntables and other servicing tracks. While the Big Boys were capable of hauling passenger trains, they rarely saw regular passenger duties.

The Big Boy was a steam locomotive born in the early days of the mass-produced diesel-electric, and it represented one of the final achievements of the steam era. Electro-Motive had successfully debuted its FT two years earlier, and by the time the Big Boy was in action, many lines were operating quartets of FTs on freights. A quartet of colorfully painted FTs might be able to start a heavy freight easier than a Big Boy, but once moving, the big steam locomotive could quickly outperform its internal combustion competition. Like many modern steam designs, the Big Boys were equipped with roller bearings on drivers and some reciprocating parts. The cylinders were integrally cast with the bed of the locomotive. Many earlier large locomotives fell short when it came to performance, yet this was not true of the Big Boy. Its boiler had ample steam capacity. One of the most notable features of the locomotive to the observer were the enormous steam pipes that fed the engines. These were much larger than on most articulated locomotives, and were designed for high capacity to give the locomotive maximum power. Although some UP steam locomotives were oil fired, the Big Boys were primarily coal burners.

Union Pacific eventually received a total of 25 Big Boys from Alco, some of which arrived during the height of American involvement in World War II, an event that placed unparalleled stress on the American railroad network. Locomotives of all kinds were at a premium, and Union Pacific made good use of its 4-8-8-4s hauling freight. They were often assigned to heavy "Fruit Blocks"—solid trains of agricultural produce originating in California for consumption in eastern and midwestern cities. These trains were very heavy, and because of the perishable load they carried, they were expedited over the railroad on priority schedules. These runs were not as fast as passenger train movements, but were nearly as tightly scheduled.

Shortly after their debut, the Big Boys were surpassed in weight by Chesapeake & Ohio's massive 2-6-6-6 Alleghenies—a little-known fact often missed by historians. Though it was a relatively rare machine, the Big Boy is one of the best remembered. They outlived most of their steam-driven kin, hauling trains over Sherman Hill until 1958. Today eight of the locomotives are preserved around the country. Perhaps someday one will run again.

Photographer Robert Hale, known for his pan shots of steam locomotives, captured a pair of Big Boys racing along with a freight near Cheyenne, Wyoming, in the mid-1950s. The Big Boys were capable of speeds up to 70 mph. *Photo by Robert Hale, Jay Williams collection*

Built in the early 1940s to move trains over the Wasatch grades east of Ogden, Utah, in later years the Big Boys were associated with UP's Sherman Hill grade, west of Cheyenne, where photographers came from around the world to see the enormous locomotive hard at work. Seen in a classic silhouette, Big Boy No. 4010 ascends Sherman Hill. *Photographer unknown, Richard Jay Solomon collection*

READING T-1

Reading 2102 negotiates a lightweight branch line in rural Pennsylvania. This is a heavy engine for such a light line; it weighs 441,300 lbs. Reading's famous T-1s were designed for heavy freight service, but they are best remembered for their late-era excursion work. Richard Jay Solomon

Reading 2102 takes in the spring sun in May 1964. The Reading's T-1s entertained thousands of enthusiasts in the late 1950s and early 1960s hauling Iron Horse Rambles. These trips, like so many other excursions, gave people the chance to experience big steam up close. *Richard Jay Solomon*

READING T-1

The Reading Company was an amalgam of eastern Pennsylvania anthracite railroads, the most prominent of which was the Philadelphia & Reading. Unlike some of the anthracite roads, which had expanded their reach to Buffalo and beyond, Reading had remained largely focused in its traditional geographic area, building just far enough to meet connections with which it interchanged its coal. To the west it went as far as Hagerstown, Maryland, where it connected with the Western Maryland and Norfolk & Western. To the east it reached Port Reading, near Perth Amboy, New Jersey, and had trackage rights over the Central Railroad of New Jersey to Jersey City for its passenger trains. Despite its small scope, it operated an intensive system, characterized by multiple-track mainlines, complex signaling, heavy freight traffic, and dense suburban passenger service. Its freight lines crossed numerous mountain grades, including some of the steepest in the East.

Unlike most American lines, which used soft bituminous coal for locomotive fuel, Reading used hard anthracite and anthracite culm (coal waste). This was a logical choice because Reading controlled large tracts of Pennsylvania's anthracite region, making this type of coal cheap and plentiful. Anthracite's hard, slow-burning characteristics required a different type locomotive firebox than softer coal. Because anthracite took much longer to ignite, and burned more slowly and hotter, locomotives that used it needed a larger firebox grate. In 1877, Philadelphia & Reading's general manager, John E. Wootten, designed a firebox with a wide grate that provided lots of area to spread the anthracite culm. Reading's subsequent locomotives were characterized

by this distinctive design. In many instances, the Wootten firebox was so wide it proved impractical to place the engineer's cab at its traditional location at the back of the locomotive. Instead, it was situated toward the middle of the boiler, leaving just a short exposed platform at the back of the locomotive for the fireman. This unusual humpback locomotive type, commonly known as a "Camelback" or a "Mother Hubbard," was very popular on the Reading and other anthracite haulers. After the turn of the twentieth century, Reading adapted the Wootten firebox for use on locomotives with a conventional orientation. In later years, Reading moved away from anthracite in favor of softer coal, but retained the wide firebox design.

The Reading Company was a progressive line, quick to adopt new technology. It had electrified its suburban passenger routes around Philadelphia, and was one of the first American lines to adopt the diesel-electric as a switching locomotive, buying boxcabs in the late 1920s, many years before diesels were popular elsewhere. However, Reading remained loyal to coal burning steam locomotives much later than its neighbors. By the mid-twentieth century, it was one of the last American railroads to build its own steam locomotives, a trait it shared with other heavy coal hauling railroads, such as the Pennsylvania Railroad, Norfolk & Western, and Illinois Central. In its Reading, Pennsylvania, shops, the company constructed more than 600 locomotives.

At the end of World War II, when most American lines were gearing up for the conversion from steam power to diesel, Reading bucked the trend by building more steam locomotives. It adopted a very modern type, despite its relatively traditional steam roster. During the 1920s and 1930s, when superpowered steam had largely superseded earlier types, Reading had stuck with tried and true steam designs. But in 1945, it decided that the 4-8-4 was well suited to its freight needs, and 18 years after that wheel arrangement had debuted on Northern Pacific, Santa Fe, and Canadian National, Reading set out to build a fleet of 4-8-4s. Rather than build its 4-8-4s from scratch, it used the boilers and fireboxes from its powerful I-10sa 2-8-0 Consolidation types as a foundation. The

I-10sa was an extraordinarily powerful Consolidation, equaling the output of many other lines' 2-8-2 Mikados and even a few 2-10-2 Santa Fe types, so its big boiler was a good starting point for a larger design. Reading lengthened the boiler and replaced the I-10sa's 61-inch drivers with modern 70-inch drivers, which used a Boxpok disc wheel design instead of the traditional spoked wheel. Disc drivers had proven their worth on superpower during the 1930s. Reading's 4-8-4 was designated "T-1" in accordance with its alpha numeric classification system that dated back to the turn of the century. In the steam era, each railroad used its own classification system, so Reading's T-1 had no relation to locomotives on other lines, such as Pennsylvania's T1 Duplex (see page 49).

Reading's T-1s were not the most powerful, the fastest, or the most significant 4-8-4s, but they were comparable to 4-8-4s operated by other anthracite roads. Like 4-8-4s built for Lehigh Valley, and some for Lackawanna, the T-1s were for heavy freight service and thus equipped with relatively small drivers, just 70 inches in diameter. In the early 1920s, 63-inch drivers were a standard size for freight work. By the end of the decade, locomotives designed for fast freight were often equipped with 69-inch drivers. The need for faster locomotives pushed the size of the drivers up. Dual-service 4-8-4s, such as New York Central's Niagara, were built with 75-inch drivers, while passenger service 4-8-4s, such as SP's famous GS-4 "Daylights," were often equipped with 79- or 80-inch drivers.

Thirty T-1s roamed Reading's mainlines, hauling through freight and working in coal service. They operated over Reading's many mountain grades, conquering Locust Summit and Buck Mountain, and toiling over the 3.3 percent Frackville Grade. The T-1's freight career was unusually short. By the late 1940s the Reading Company had forsaken its steam policy, and begun to take a significant interest in diesels. The T-1s were used in regular service for just six years, although they remained on the roster for extra moves and peak traffic until spring 1956. In their last years, the T-1s worked a variety of assignments out of Shamokin, St. Clair, Tamaqua, and Gordon, Pennsylvania, serving as both head-end power and as rear-end "pushers." In early 1956, Reading loaned a half-dozen T-1s to the power-hungry Pennsylvania Railroad, which employed them on its Susquehanna Division.

Had Reading scrapped all 30 T-1s after it concluded regular steam operations, this class of locomotives in all probability would have remained relatively obscure examples of late-era steam. Thankfully, five T-1s survived for a few more years as excursion locomotives. On October 25, 1959, Reading operated the first of its popular Iron Horse Rambles with T-1 No. 2124. During the next four years, Reading operated more than 40 steam excursions with its remaining T-1s, Numbers 2100, 2101, 2102, 2123, and 2124. These excursions covered much of Reading's complex network, carrying thousands of railroad enthusiasts. Sadly, by 1964, Reading ended the steam rambles. Four of the T-1s survived and still exist today. One T-1 was among the three locomotives used to haul the American Freedom Train, which celebrated the American Bicentennial in the mid-1970s. Recently, T-1 No. 2100 made its way to St. Thomas, Ontario, where it is housed and occasionally displayed. T-1 No. 2102 is occasionally operated by the Blue Mountain & Reading, a shortline railroad that owns several former Reading Company routes.

◄ Organized steam trips mostly operate between Memorial Day and Labor Day, which is unfortunate for photographers, because the most dramatic photos of steam are made at twilight in cold weather. On the rainy evening of November 14, 1959, a Reading Iron Horse Ramble led by T-1 No. 2124 blasts through Oak Lane Station in Philadelphia. *Richard Jay Solomon*

▲ Five of the Reading's T-1s were later assigned to excursion service, and four survive today. The 2102 is back in home territory, having been sold to the Blue Mountain & Reading in 1986. It is seen here in about 1963 on an Iron Horse Ramble. *Richard Jay Solomon*

PENNSYLVANIA T1

The Pennsylvania Railroad T1 was born too late to be properly appreciated. In a world awed by the promise of diesel-electrics, the unorthodox T1 design was considered freakish by some, unfortunate by others. On September 8, 1946, T1 No. 5535 leads the Trailblazer *at Englewood, Illinois. Within a decade it would be out of service, replaced by Electro-Motive E-units.* Photo by Kennedy, Jay Williams collection

Pennsylvania T1

A T1 was capable of racing across the flatlands at great speed but it was no match for the steep grades west of Altoona, Pennsylvania. In July 1948, one of PRR's venerable L1 2-8-2 Mikados helps a T1 make it to the summit of the Alleghenies at Gallitzin. *Photographer unknown, J. R. Quinn collection*

Despite the advent of practical diesel-electric motive power, the Pennsylvania Railroad pursued a nonconventional vision of the future and designed what it hoped would be the future of the American steam locomotive. Although Electro-Motive had demonstrated that diesels could haul passenger trains over a great distance at high speed, PRR felt that steam power could match and exceed that performance. So in the late 1930s PRR teamed with the three large steam builders to dream up a new supersteam locomotive. What they designed was PRR's famous S1, a futuristic streamlined monster with fantastic proportions and great power. It was a Duplex type, meaning it had two complete sets of running gear on a single non-articulated frame.

The Duplex's divided drive was intended to reduce the length of the piston thrusts, in order to lessen the weight of drive rods and other reciprocating gear and thus minimize the effects of dynamic augment—the damaging pounding forces caused by imbalances in reciprocating parts. PRR's S1 was not the first Duplex—in the mid-1930s, Baltimore & Ohio had built one as an experiment. PRR was very proud of its S1 and displayed it at the 1939 New York World's Fair, where it rolled away on a treadmill. While thrilling to watch, the enormous locomotive soon proved

impractical for road use because its long wheelbase restricted its operation east of Pittsburgh, and it was too long to fit on most turntables. The PRR was not easily defeated by such nominal oversights, so they designed another Duplex type with more reasonable proportions. By the time the railroad was ready to build its new Duplex, American involvement in World War II resulted in strict limits on new locomotive designs, and PRR had to obtain special permission from the War Production Board to build two experimental Duplex prototypes. Where the S1 had used a 6-4-4-6 wheel arrangement, the new prototypes were 4-4-4-4s, PRR's answer to the successful 4-8-4 Northern arrangement. They were classed and designed for 100-mile per hour operation with an 880-ton passenger train. Unlike the S1, the T1 prototypes were a more manageable size and conformed to most of the railroad's weight and length restrictions.

The two experimental T1s were built at Altoona, Pennsylvania, and shrouded in distinctive streamlined shrouds created by the famous industrial designer Raymond Loewy. (Loewy also worked on the streamlining on the GG1 [see page 138], the K4s ["s" for superheated] Pacifics, and the aforementioned S1.) Loewy gave the T1 a mean looking "shark-nose" profile—a design later adapted by Baldwin for its early road diesels (see page 70)—that incorporated a number of art deco styling features consistent with PRR's image. The T1s were painted in PRR's Brunswick green, a dark color used on the GG1. They featured bright red PRR keystones on their pilots and tenders and handsome gold striping, which, when it was clean, gave PRR equipment a look of imperial elegance.

During the war, PRR put its T1 prototypes through extensive testing at its Altoona test plant—one of the few scientific steam locomotive research facilities in the world. Meanwhile they were featured prominently in advertising that promoted the war effort and PRR's fantastic visions of the future of steam. After the war, PRR ordered 50 T1s, 25 from its own Altoona Works, and 25 from Baldwin, a longtime builder of PRR locomotives; Baldwin built road numbers 5525 to 5549. The production models featured a slightly different streamlining treatment that retained the basic stylistic elements of the prototypes, but lacked elegance. The tapered nose was less pronounced, and the shrouded skirting was minimized for ease of maintenance.

The T1 was intended to eliminate the need for double-heading K4s Pacific types on heavy passenger trains. Thus, a single T1 was intended to do the work of two K4s Pacifics. They were assigned to work long-distance passenger trains from west of the end of electrification at Harrisburg to Chicago and St. Louis. The T1 embodied all the features of the most modern steam: 80-inch drivers, roller bearings, high boiler pressure, and even the recently developed poppet valves instead of more conventional piston valves. In terms of sheer speed, the T1s could outperform just about anything else on level track. There are tales of them racing across Indiana and Ohio at speeds in excess of 100 miles per hour!

Although we will never know for sure, they might have been the fastest steam locomotives ever built. No one alive knows their top limit.

Sadly, PRR's vision of the future fell short. Although a magnificent machine and capable of great speeds, the T1's failing was reliability. They embodied too many innovations too quickly, and didn't have the time for refinement, when the diesels were already at the doorstep, fast, efficient, and ready to go. Furthermore, other railroads built more reliable modern steam using highly refined conventional designs. New York Central, which had considered the Duplex, built its famous 4-8-4 Niagaras instead. And by most accounts, these locomotives gave superlative performances. Norfolk & Western operated its J class, high-performance 4-8-4s, known for their exceptional reliability.

Despite all of PRR's best intentions, the T1s suffered headaches from flawed engineering. The innovative poppet valves resulted in numerous failures, while the T1s also suffered from inadequate steaming potential, which has been attributed to a small firebox grate. One of the most alarming problems was a defect in the suspension system that caused one engine to slip when a locomotive was traveling at speed. The result was a severe loss of power that made for rough train handling. Also, Loewy's aesthetically stunning streamlining had a tendency to deflect smoke back into the cab, which annoyed the crew. Certainly these problems could have been solved given enough time. PRR, however, had had a change of management and followed the conventional path by adopting the diesel instead of fixing the T1s. Steam was dead, and the T1s had short careers as premier mainline passenger power. Some were later bumped to freight. All were scrapped. Even less successful was PRR's freight Duplex, the infamous Q2. Massive, powerful machines, they only lasted about three years in service.

Historians have long speculated why PRR followed the course that it did, and why it invested so much in unproven technology so late in the steam era. The answer probably lies in the PRR's belief in itself, and its deeply felt ties to the power of coal and of steam locomotives. Despite the superior efficiency of the diesel, some in the industry felt that steam still had a place. In the end the diesel won out.

Top: The T1 5517 was photographed on a clear cold morning at Englewood Union Station in February 1947. *Photographer unknown, Jay Williams collection*

Center: Pennsylvania Railroad T1 No. 5502 was built by the railroad's company shops at Altoona in November 1945. It was photographed in Chicago in July 1948. Notice the lack of stylized portholes on the pilot. Many T1s lost bits of their shrouding in later years, presumably for ease of maintenance. *Photographer unknown, Jay Williams collection*

Bottom: The PRR's T1 No. 5517 basks in the sun at St. Louis, Missouri. The Pennsylvania had 52 of these locomotives, making them the most numerous single class of streamlined steam in the United States. While PRR preserved many examples of its steam power, none of its late-era steams survived. All the T1s were cut up for scrap. *Photographer unknown, J. R. Quinn Collection*

DIESEL POWER

In 1994, Southern Pacific and Wisconsin Central initiated an arrangement to haul iron ore between Superior, Wisconsin, and Geneva Steel in Utah. This move warranted SP's most modern power and for a short time called for trios of DASH 9s, as seen here in October 1994 south of Teresa, Wisconsin. *Brian Solomon*

The United States was one of the first countries to develop the diesel locomotive. The first commercially successful diesel was a small boxcab switcher built by a consortium of Alco, General Electric, and Ingersoll-Rand for the Central Railroad of New Jersey in 1925. From that point on, the diesel concept gradually gained acceptance by American railroads, and it was developed into a host of different locomotive designs. American diesel locomotives are diesel-electrics, meaning a diesel engine is used to generate electricity to power traction motors that turn the wheels. In other countries, diesel-hydraulic locomotives have been used, which employ a hydraulic transmission system in place of the electrical one.

Several diesel-electric manufacturers emerged in the first few decades of commercial diesel production. Logically, the two largest steam locomotive manufacturers, Alco and Baldwin, were important players in the early years. However, the most important force in developing and promoting the use of diesel-electric locomotives was General Motors' Electro-Motive Division (which was known as the Electro-Motive Corporation until 1939). During the 1930s, Electro-Motive developed and sold road diesels in every major category of the

locomotive market. Following World War II, EMD quickly emerged as the leading diesel-electric locomotive manufacturer. In the decade following the war, railroads quickly converted their operations from steam to diesel and bought thousands of new locomotives. Four major builders competed for locomotive sales during this period: EMD, Alco, Baldwin, and diesel-engine manufacturer Fairbanks-Morse. By the time American railroads had completed their dieselization, only EMD and Alco remained in the locomotive market. In 1960 General Electric introduced its own line of heavy-haul road locomotives. During the 1960s, there was competition between EMD, Alco, and GE. In 1969 Alco dropped out of the market, and since 1970 the majority of American diesel-electric locomotives have been built by either EMD or GE.

Alco's Canadian subsidiary, Montreal Locomotive Works, continued to supply locomotives to the Canadian market for another decade after Alco discontinued its locomotive line. MLW eventually exited the market, and conveyed its line to Bombardier, which only manufactured locomotives for a few years.

In the 1990s, Morrison-Knudsen attempted to enter the new heavy-haul locomotive market without much success.

When discussing locomotives, the diesel engine usually refers to the powerplant inside the locomotive, as opposed to the locomotive itself. For example, an EMD GP9 uses a 16-cylinder 567C diesel engine. The output of the diesel locomotive is often measured in horsepower, although sometimes the tractive effort is also used as a measure of a diesel's hauling capabilities.

Distinguishing different diesel locomotives can be difficult. From a technological standpoint, what makes one locomotive different from another has more to do with what goes on beneath the hood, rather than superficial exterior appearances. Two models that may look entirely different on the outside, may be very similar inside, and vice versa. For example Baldwin's DR-4-4-15 was built with two very different carbody styles, including the so-called shark-nose style. The shark-nose style was dreamed up to help distinguish Baldwin diesels in the competitive postwar market, and was used for several different locomotive models and not just the DR-4-4-15. In another situation, General Electric's DASH 9-44CW, and its AC4400CW look virtually identical on the outside, yet employ two entirely different traction systems. The DASH 9 uses conventional direct-current traction, while the

AC4400CW uses a new state-of-the-art three-phase alternating-current traction system. When AC traction was first introduced in the mid-1990s, it was described as the most significant change in locomotive technology since the switch from steam to diesel. So despite their similar appearance, the DASH 9-44CW and AC4400CW are quite different machines. This is one reason a few very similar-looking models have been included in the book. To the casual observer, General Electric's DASH 9, and its modern AC6000CW may seen remarkably similar, but as to their diesel locomotive technology, looks are deceiving!

The fact boxes for the diesel locomotives generally illustrate specific models relevant to the section. In some instances the fact box may highlight just one model representative of a group of similar models discussed in the text. For example, the fact box for the Electro-Motive F-Unit covers the F7 model, but it provides a nice overview of EMD's several F-unit models. The item listing the number of locomotives built only reflects the North American market (United States, Canada, and Mexico) and doesn't take into consideration locomotives sold overseas. The sole exception is the EMD Class 66, which is an export model not built for domestic use.

Far left: A cab close-up of CSX AC6000CW No. 613 at Palmer, Massachusetts. The significance of modern AC locomotives lies out of sight, inside the locomotive. Exterior features such as the safety cab and other superfluous trappings are common to both modern AC and DC traction locomotives. *Brian Solomon*

Top right: In July 2000, a Class 66 sits on a side track at Warrington in England. By American standards the Class 66 seems quite compact, but the locomotive is enormous relative to some traditional British designs. *Brian Solomon*

Lower right: Central Vermont's S-4 switcher, No. 8081, had just been shopped and painted for K&L Feeds of Franklin, Connecticut, when this photo was made at the CV's New London Yard in February 1988. Built in 1955, the locomotive spent most of its life working on the CV in northern Vermont. *Brian Solomon*

ELECTRO-MOTIVE F UNIT

An FL9 in a heritage New Haven livery at Waterbury, Connecticut, in 1993. Among the most interesting and unusual variations of Electro-Motive's F series were the 60 FL9s built for New Haven between 1956 and 1960. These dual-mode, diesel-electric/electric locomotives were designed to operate using either the 16-cylinder 567 engine or from direct-current third rail. Brian Solomon

In the 1950s, EMD F-units were the most common variety of diesel-electric locomotive in America. Two Chesapeake & Ohio F7As lead a loaded coal train through Covington, Kentucky, on July 28, 1958. The F7 was rated at 1,500 horsepower, giving these two locomotives just 3,000 horsepower. Today most heavy freight trains are assigned upward of 10,000 horsepower. *Richard Jay Solomon*

ELECTRO-MOTIVE F-UNIT

In November 1939, as Europe was sinking into war, General Motors' Electro-Motive Corporation (soon to be reorganized as its Electro-Motive Division, or EMD) debuted its latest diesel-electric locomotive, the FT. Just as World War II would irreversibly redraw political boundaries on the continent, EMC's F-unit would forever change American railway infrastructure.

During the 1930s, Electro-Motive had refined diesel-electric technology to the point where it could compete with steam. In 1934, the first diesel-powered streamliners demonstrated their suitability as road locomotives. Subsequent designs showed that the diesel was an effective passenger hauler, as well as a practical yard switcher. However, the largest, most significant market for the new technology was in hauling heavy freight. Whisking a lightweight passenger train over the road was one thing; moving a long, heavy freight was something else altogether. Since the railroads earned most of their revenue from freight, they had a serious interest in a practical road diesel. General Motors saw an enormous business opportunity in freight locomotives. By the late 1930s, freight traffic had begun a steady recovery since the lows of the Great Depression, yet most railroads were saddled with fleets of antiquated steam locomotives, many more than 20 years old. Some lines had not ordered any new locomotives since the 1920s, and were ready to invest in new power.

The four-unit F set comprised two "A" unit cabs, and two "B" unit cabless boosters in an A-B-B-A configuration. Each unit used a 16-cylinder 567 diesel engine to generate 1,350 horsepower, giving

the entire set a 5,400-horsepower rating. This was enough power to match that produced by many of the most modern steam locomotives. While some steam may have had higher total output, steam could not match the FT's enormous starting tractive effort. One of the principal performance advantages of diesel-electric motive power over steam is diesel's ability to apply maximum power from a standstill. A steam locomotive only achieves maximum power when it is moving at speed.

The FT was a handsome machine. Like Electro-Motive's E-units, it featured a streamlined full carbody. But unlike the early Es, which had a long slanted front end, the FT sported a new look. It was the first model to use the rounded "Bull Dog" nose, which would become one of the famous faces in American railroading. The locomotives ran on a newly designed Blomberg two-axle truck, which incorporated a suspension system similar to that employed on the A1A six-axle Blomberg truck designed for the E-unit. (An A1A truck has a three-axle design, in which only the outside axles are powered. The inside axle is intended to help distribute the weight of the locomotive over a greater number of wheels. The A1A style of truck was popular with several early passenger locomotive designs, but has largely fallen out of favor.)

In 1940, Electro-Motive sent its four-unit, streamlined FT demonstrator on an epic 11-month, 84,000-mile tour of American railroads. The demonstrator covered 20 different lines, hauling a variety of trains in different conditions. In short, the FT accomplished what it set out to do, and the railroads were impressed. By the end of the year, Electro-Motive was already building production FTs. One of its first large customers was Santa Fe, which had experience with Electro-Motive's E-units and was already impressed with the diesel-electric's capabilities. However, just as the FT was starting to get a toehold in the locomotive market, the United States entered World War II in December 1941. The dramatic increase in industrial activity in support of the war effort had a profound affect on the nation's railroads, and on the locomotive market. Traffic levels soared to new highs. Railroads were suddenly deluged with traffic and scrambling for locomotives, after years of minimal purchases of new locomotives during the Depression. At the same time, the War Production Board placed severe restrictions on locomotive production and development. Electro-Motive was the only company permitted to produce large numbers of road diesels, yet its production was strictly limited. Some lines were forced to order steam locomotives when they would have preferred diesels. Despite the advent of the war restrictions, Electro-Motive sold 1,096 FTs (both cabs and boosters), making it by far the most popular diesel model at the time.

The war had a refining effect on the F-unit that many authorities claim gave GM a distinct market advantage. Although it was not permitted to implement major design alterations during the war in order to comply with regulations mandating parts compatibility, Electro-Motive was able to continue its research and learn from four years of FT fleets in demanding service. Furthermore, by the end of the war, the railroads were starving for new locomotives. The aged fleets of steam locomotives were suffering from low maintenance, overuse, and obsolescence. Electro-Motive was faced with a host of competitors after the war, but it had the best product and quickly commanded the largest market share of new road diesel orders.

Immediately after the war, it introduced an improved line of F-units. First there was an interim F2 model, built in 1946 while Electro-Motive was preparing for mass-production of its F3 model. The F3 was slightly more powerful and markedly more reliable than its predecessor. The F3 was rated at 1,500 horsepower, giving a four-unit

The FP7 was 4 feet longer than a basic F7A to accommodate an extra steam generator capacity needed for passenger service. Rock Island FP7 410 rests in the afternoon sun at Blue Island, Illinois, on July 18, 1958. Rock Island was known for its varied and colorful paint schemes. *Richard Jay Solomon*

On May 21, 1976, two F7As lead an ore train at Cleveland, Ohio. By the mid-1970s, the once-omnipresent F-unit had become something of a novelty on American Class I railroads, and by the early 1980s, most Fs had been traded in for more modern power. *Photo by Bill Dechau, Doug Eisele collection*

Bangor & Aroostook was the last New England line to operate a significant fleet of F3s in regular service. No. 42 had an auxiliary generator to give heating and lighting power to the passenger cars. As a result, it was often polished up and assigned to the railroad's business train, as seen here at Millinocket, Maine, in May 1979. *George S. Pitarys*

set a 6,000-horsepower rating. Instead of belt and mechanically driven fans and appliances as on the FT, the F3 used electrical power. Also unlike the FT sets, which were semi-permanently coupled in A-B configurations, the F3s were fitted with normal couplers that gave the railroads greater flexibility in assigning the locomotives.

In 1949, Electro-Motive introduced its most popular F-unit model, the widely acclaimed F7. Externally, this locomotive closely resembled the F3, but internally it embodied a host of performance and reliability improvements. The F7 had a better traction motor design, giving it greater starting traction effort and better short time ratings, allowing it to operate longer under maximum load. A new fuel injection design allowed the locomotive to burn lower (and

cheaper) grades of fuel. The FP7 model was a slightly longer version, with a steam generator for passenger service—thus the "P" in the designation. The F7s were one of Electro-Motive's greatest successes, selling an astonishing 3,849 units to North American railroads.

In 1954, Electro-Motive brought out the slightly more powerful F9, replacing the F7. The F9 was rated at 1,750 horsepower in order to compete with the higher output offered by other locomotive builders. An FP9 variation was also produced. Between 1956 and 1960, a specialized diesel-electric/electric version was built for the New Haven—the FL9. This dual-powered locomotive was equipped with third rail shoes to draw current from electrified lines between New York's Grand Central Terminal and Woodlawn in The Bronx, and through the East River Tunnels to Penn Station. It featured an unusual B-A1A wheel arrangement to comply with weight restrictions on its intended route to Grand Central Terminal.

The F9 was the last and one of the poorest-selling F-unit designs—just 384 units were built. The reason for this is simple. By the mid-1950s, American railroads had turned away from full carbody models, instead preferring to purchase road switcher types.

The F-unit was the ubiquitous symbol of dieselization. It could be found everywhere from the northern woods of Maine to the coasts of southern California. With a handful of exceptions, nearly every major railroad in America operated F-units at one time or another. Their numbers started to dwindle in the 1960s as new, more powerful road switchers were introduced. By the 1980s, the F-unit had largely faded from the American scene. A few soldiered on, running on isolated routes, commuter lines, tourist railways, or in a variety of modified forms. A number were rebuilt for modern suburban commuter service. Others were converted to road slugs, snowplow power cars, or rebuilt as road switchers. A number have been preserved, including the pioneering FT demonstrator.

At noon on July 5, 1994, an inordinate amount of noise shook the clear Montana air east of Cyr. What could make such a sound? No SD40-2 or SD45 makes so much noise. What's this . . . F-units on a mainline freight in 1994? The Burlington Northern executive F9s lead intermodal train No. 21 bound for Seattle over the Montana Rail Link. *Brian Solomon*

ALCO "S" SWITCHERS

A Genesee & Wyoming Alco S-4 switcher idles near the railroad's Retsof, New York, shops in January 1988. The AAR type A truck and large radiator fan at the front of the locomotive identify this engine as a 1,000-horsepower S-4, Brian Solomon

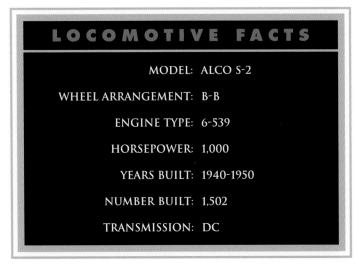

ALCO "S" SWITCHERS

▲ New York Central operated the largest fleet of Alco diesels in the United States—not surprising, considering Alco had been Central's primary steam locomotive builder. New York Central S-1 No. 858 and a sibling rest at Central's North Bergen Yards in the New Jersey Meadows on April 13, 1958. The combination of Blount trucks and a small radiator give this away as a 660-horsepower S-1. *Richard Jay Solomon*

▶ The larger radiator is a feature of the S-2 and S-4 switchers. These locomotives required more cooling as a result of the turbocharged 539 engine, which generated 1,000 horsepower. *Brian Solomon*

LOCOMOTIVE FACTS

MODEL: ALCO S-2

WHEEL ARRANGEMENT: B-B

ENGINE TYPE: 6-539

HORSEPOWER: 1,000

YEARS BUILT: 1940-1950

NUMBER BUILT: 1,502

TRANSMISSION: DC

Alco, the steam locomotive manufacturer, was one of the earliest builders of commercially successful diesel-electric locomotives. Most of the early diesel-electrics served as switching locomotives. By 1936, Alco had built more than 30 diesel switchers. The first examples were boxcab models, such as those it built in conjunction with GE and Ingersoll-Rand in the 1920s. Its later models used a hood configuration inspired by Westinghouse's "visibility cab." Where the Westinghouse locomotives used a tapered notch in the body of the locomotive to give crews a better view, Alco employed a narrow hood over the engine and other primary components with walkways for access on each side of the hood. The driving cab occupied the full width of the locomotive, giving the engineer a good view fore and aft without having to change his position. This was a better arrangement for switching than on the early boxcabs, which required two cabs, one at each end of the locomotive.

In 1934—the same year that the first Electro-Motive–powered streamliners debuted—Alco hired well-known industrial designer Otto Kuhler to clean up the outward appearance of its 600-horsepower switcher. Among other changes, he raised the hood level to match the roofline of the cab and added recessed headlights for a smoother look. These switchers used a new four-wheeled truck design, known as the "Blount" truck after its designer. Diesel builders adopted new industry standards in 1936, leading Alco to introduce a new line of 660-horsepower and 900-horsepower diesel switchers using the Kuhler-designed profile. Today these switchers are known as HH660 and HH900 models, the "HH" standing for "high hood," which distinguishes them from later models.

Alco's more compact Model 539 engine permitted frame mounting, allowing Alco to lower the hood on its diesel switcher designs. This made for a more balanced-looking machine and resulted in clearer forward visibility for the crew. The 539 engine came in two distinct varieties, normally aspirated and turbocharged. In 1940 Alco introduced two new low-hood switchers that incorporated six-cylinder versions of the new engines. The new model designations used an "S" to indicate "switcher." Alco's S-1 used the naturally aspirated engine, rated at 660 horsepower, while the S-2 used the turbocharged version generating 1,000 horsepower.

During World War II, the War Production Board largely restricted Alco's production to switchers, but the company sold a great many of them during this period. By 1950, Alco had built more than 2,000 S-1s and S-2s for North American service, the more powerful, turbocharged S-2 being more popular. Externally, the S-1 and S-2 appeared very similar, with a balanced utilitarian design that was basic, but not unpleasant to look at. Both models used Blount trucks and the new low-hood design. They measured 45 feet, 5.75 inches long, and featured cabs with nicely rounded profiles. The only obvious identifying feature to distinguish the S1 from the S2 is the length of the radiator at the front of the locomotive. Since the turbocharged S2 needed greater radiator capacity than the normally aspirated S-1, its radiator is longer. The S-2's radiator measures about half the length of the Blount truck, while the S-1's is less than half the truck length.

In 1950, after a decade of S switcher production, Alco upgraded its line, introducing the S-3 in place of the S-1, and the S-4 in place of the S-2. The primary spotting difference between these newer switchers and their older kin was a common American Association of Railroads (AAR) truck design instead of the Blount truck. The S-3 model was discontinued in 1953, but the S-4 continued until 1961.

◄ Seaboard Coast Line Alco S-2 No. 50 is seen on March 26, 1976, leading Amtrak's *Floridian* to the wash racks at Hialeah, Florida. The Seaboard Coast Line was formed from a merger between two longtime competitors, the Seaboard Air Line and the Atlantic Coast Line, which vied for traffic between Richmond, Virginia, and Florida. The SCL became part of the Family Lines in the 1970s, and later part of the gigantic CSX in the 1980s. *Doug Eisele*

▼ The distinctive Blount truck, named for its designer, was only used on pre-1950 Alco switchers. It featured a 96-inch wheelbase. By the year 2000, operative diesel locomotives with Blount trucks were rarer than steam engines, yet a few survive. *Brian Solomon*

Montreal Locomotive Works, Alco's Canadian subsidiary, built limited numbers of S-10 and S-11 switchers for the Canadian market that used the 660-horsepower engine, and shared common attributes with the S-1 and S-3. It also constructed S-12s that used the 1,000-horsepower 539 engine. (MLW's S-12 model should not be confused with Baldwin's locomotive with the same model designation, also built as a switcher in the mid-1950s.) The combined production of all three of these Canadian switcher models totaled less than 100 locomotives, making them far less common than the more widely used American switcher models.

Although Alco developed the more powerful 241 and 244 engines, it continued to use its older (and more reliable) 539 engine in its switchers. In the early 1950s, Alco developed a new, more powerful, and more reliable engine, the 251, to supersede the 244 design, which had been plagued with reliability problems. The first production locomotives to receive the 251 engine were the 800-horsepower S-5 switchers, built in June 1954. Boston & Maine, the only large road to buy this model, ordered six of the seven built. The following year Alco brought out its S-6 design, which used a refined 251A engine that produced 900 horsepower. This model sold better than the S-5, but didn't achieve the widespread sales enjoyed by the earlier models. This was partially an effect of the declining need for new diesel switchers by American railroads. The largest demand for diesel switchers had occurred during the height of the steam-to-diesel transition. By the mid-1950s most American lines had completed their dieselization, and since switch engines generally enjoy long service lives, the railroads had little need to order more. Both the S-5 and S-6 shared the same body style, employing a slightly different configuration than the earlier S models. The radiator faced forward, making for a more boxy front end. The exhaust stack, set toward the front, used a straighter design. In Canada, MLW built the S-13, which used a 251C engine to generate 1,000 horsepower. Both this model and other later MLW switchers used the same body style as the S-5 and S-6. All of these later models used the AAR-style truck.

Alco switchers were among the most common first-generation diesels. They could be found all across North America, working an array of duties. They hauled branch line local freights, switched out freight yards, organized passenger consists at major terminals and coach yards, and wandered back alleys and industrial parks gathering freight traffic. New York State, in particular was a bastion for Alco products long after they disappeared from other regions. This is partly attributable to Alco's location in Schenectady in upstate New York. Many New York short lines continued to operate Schenectady products more than 20 years after Alco ceased production.

Despite its ubiquitous nature, the Alco switcher seemed to elude photographers and chronologists until they had practically disappeared from American rails. While S switchers were occasionally committed to film, they were largely ignored in favor of more flashy subjects on the main line. When scrutinizing old photographs, one will often see a Blount-truck Alco in the background, while the main subject—be it the *20th Century Limited*, or a fast freight on the Union Pacific—looms large in the foreground. Today Alco switchers are sought after by enthusiasts as curiosities and antiques. Despite their age, a handful can be found working on short lines, many long past their 50th birthday!

NEW YORK CENTRAL SYSTEM

8357
DRS-6
P&LE

ALCO RS-3

▲ *Battenkill Railroad 605 works weed-grown tracks once owned by the Delaware & Hudson at Eagle Bridge, New York, where this short-line interchanges freight traffic with Guilford Rail System. This RS-3 is among the last active survivors of the 1,400 units that Alco built between 1950 and 1956.* Brian Solomon

◄ *The semi-streamlined hood of Alco's early 1950s road-switchers is among the best remembered designs from the first generation era. Pittsburgh & Lake Erie RS-3 8357 was the highest number of its class on the railroad's roster. It is seen here in parent New York Central's classic "lightning stripe" paint.* Richard Jay Solomon

Today the RS-3 is a rare bird among the vast fleets of modern six-motor, high-horsepower safety cab diesels, of which only a few survive. The chugging sounds of an aged 244 engine resound on the morning of September 6, 2000, at Eagle Bridge, New York, as Battenkill Railroad RS-3 605 rolls across the Hoosic River. *Brian Solomon*

ALCO RS-3

The three earliest standard diesel-electric types were switchers, road passenger units, and road freight units. The switcher was introduced as a boxcab, and later evolved as a hooded diesel, while the two road locomotive types tended to feature full carbody designs and streamlined styling. Alco was one of the earliest commercial builders of diesel switchers. In the 1920s it was part of a consortium with General Electric and Ingersoll-Rand that built the first successful boxcabs. In the 1930s, Alco worked with GE building a commercial line of light diesel switchers. While the streamlined passenger trains of the mid-1930s are recognized as spurring a national interest in diesel-electric motive power, these flashy passenger diesels represented only a small part of the diesel market, compared to the fairly large numbers of diesel switchers sold at the same time.

Typically switchers would work on light track in yards and industrial areas, and only stray out onto the mainline for switching drills and local work. In 1941, Alco expanded its switcher design into a locomotive that was intended for light road assignments in addition to basic switching. This new type was seen as something of a hybrid type and called a "road switcher." Later the type was designated RS-1, "RS" signifying "road switcher." The RS-1 closely resembled Alco's switchers and employed Alco's turbocharged six-cylinder 539 engine rated at 1,000 horsepower.

This new road switcher proved a versatile machine capable of handling a variety of assignments. Alco built hundreds of RS-1 road switchers during the war, many of which were designed for military use and export. Most RS-1s used a four-axle B-B wheel arrangement, standard on diesel switchers, but some were equipped with six-motor, six-axle (C) trucks, and others with four-motor, six-axle (A1A) trucks.

As World War II drew to a close, Alco prepared for a postwar diesel boom. During the war it had been working on a new diesel engine design, designated 241. Toward the end of the war, this design was abandoned prior to production, and a different design, designated 244 and based on the 241, was advanced instead. The 12-cylinder 244 was initially rated at 1,500 horsepower and entered regular production at the end of 1945. It was the preferred engine for Alco's postwar road diesel designs, while the older 539 engine was still used for switchers and RS-1 models.

In 1946, Alco introduced a new semi-streamlined four-motor road switcher, designated RS-2, that used the 244 engine. Like the RS-1, the RS-2 was adept at handling many different assignments. RS-2s could be used to switch a coach yard, work a yard local, or take the milk run, or several of them could work in tandem on a road freight. Alco was not alone in the road switcher market anymore. Baldwin and Fairbanks-Morse also introduced road switchers after the war. However, diesel-electric giant Electro-Motive expressed little interest in building road switchers in the immediate postwar period, and instead focused its production on the three standard types—switchers, road passenger units, and road freight units.

The postwar diesel market was fiercely competitive, as American railroads replaced their worn-out steam fleets. In these years, Electro-Motive was clearly the market leader, while Alco, Baldwin, F-M, and others, fought for the remainder of the business. In 1950, Alco, Baldwin, and F-M all boosted the output of their standard freight and road switcher models from 1,500 to 1,600 horsepower to give them an edge over EMD's offerings. Alco initially boosted the RS-2s to 1,600 horsepower, but in mid-1950, Alco introduced a new locomotive model, the RS-3, to reflect the increase in power and other improvements. The RS-3 debuted just as American lines were

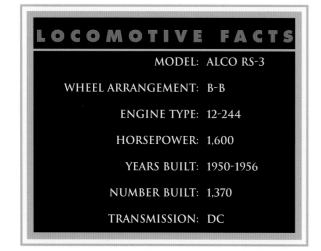

LOCOMOTIVE FACTS

MODEL: ALCO RS-3

WHEEL ARRANGEMENT: B-B

ENGINE TYPE: 12-244

HORSEPOWER: 1,600

YEARS BUILT: 1950-1956

NUMBER BUILT: 1,370

TRANSMISSION: DC

shifting their diesel emphasis from traditional full carbodies (such as the Alco FA, and EMD F-units) to road switchers. It was the right locomotive at the right time and sold very well. Road switchers had the same output as conventional carbody locomotives, yet demonstrated a number of advantages over carbody locomotives: they were cheaper to build, featured bidirectional operation, and were easier to maintain.

In 1949, EMD finally introduced its own true road switcher design, the GP7 (see page 83), which was rated at 1,500 horsepower, the same as its F3 and F7 carbody models. Although the Alco RS-3 didn't sell as well as the GP7, the RS-3 proved to be good competition for the EMD road switcher.

In the late 1940s, when most railroads initiated plans to completely dieselize their operations, they typically bought large fleets of EMD F-units, or Alco FA/FB cabs. A handful of lines waited until

the advent of the road switcher before initiating their steam-to-diesel conversion plans. The Delaware & Hudson, for example, skipped the cab-unit phase entirely, and effectively brought about dieselization with Alco road switchers. It purchased a sizable fleet of RS-3s, which it assigned to virtually every task on the railroad. Only in later years did it pick up cab-units secondhand from other lines. Delaware & Hudson's appetite for the RS-3 reflected the general popularity of Alco road switchers among eastern carriers. While a few western lines bought Alco RS-3s, the majority of them were operated by lines east of the Mississippi. New York Central, Boston & Maine, New Haven, Erie, and New Jersey Central all operated significant RS-3 fleets. The Pennsylvania Railroad had one of the largest RS-3 fleets, 45 of them equipped with steam generators for passenger service, and another 70 for freight. They were by far the most popular Alco model on PRR's diesel roster. PRR owned one unusual RS-3 type that featured a high, short hood to accommodate dynamic braking equipment and a steam generator. This locomotive, later operated by the Lehigh Valley Western Maryland, also had a high, short-hood RS-3.

Alco and its Canadian subsidiary, Montreal Locomotive Works, built more than 1,400 RS-3s between 1950 and 1956. Most were sold in the United States, but some 98 RS-3s were sold to Canada and a handful to Mexico. The RS-3 was discontinued when Alco introduced road locomotives powered by its new 251 diesel engine, a design that overcame many of the problems associated with the 244. The flawed 244 engine contributed to a relatively short life for many locomotives equipped with it. By the early 1970s, 244 Alcos were already a rare breed. In many cases, 539 Alcos, such as the RS-1, outlived newer 244 models.

A few railroads extended the service lives of RS-2s and RS-3s by rebuilding them with other engine designs. Penn Central rebuilt many of its RS-3s at its DeWitt, New York, shops (near Syracuse), substituting the more reliable Electro-Motive 567 engine. Since the EMD engine is taller than Alco's, Central's rebuilds feature an unsightly bulge on the long hood that spoiled the RS-3's classic profile. Conrail inherited RS-3 fleets from PC and other railroads, and continued the rebuilding program. Later rebuilds were done at Conrail's Altoona shops, which modified the Alco frame to accommodate the 567 engine, making for a better-looking locomotive. All of these PC/Conrail rebuilds were designated by the railroads as RS-3m models. The Katy rebuilt some RS-3s, equipping them with 567 engines and exchanging the Alco long hood with that from an EMD GP9. In the mid-1970s Morrison-Knudsen rebuilt some Delaware & Hudson RS-3s using the more reliable Alco 251 engine, while simultaneously lowering the short hood to give the operating crew a better forward view. Most RS-3s were scrapped, but a few survive today on short lines and in railroad museums.

◄ Erie-Lackawanna RS-3 1051 works at Marion, Ohio. The Alco four-cycle engine was known for its propensity to belch black smoke, and the 244 variety was among the best performers. In the years following the demise of steam locomotives, many photographers would happily settle for a smoky Alco diesel. *Photo by Bill Dechau, Doug Eisele collection*

▼ Just two Alco RS-3s were built with a high short hood, one for the Western Maryland and this one for the Pennsylvania Railroad. Originally numbered PRR 8445, this locomotive was later traded to the Lehigh Valley, and eventually operated under the Conrail name following consolidation in 1976. Under Conrail it was rebuilt at Altoona with an EMD engine. It is now preserved at Industry, New York. *Doug Eisele*

BALDWIN'S SHARKS

Delaware & Hudson's RF16 No. 1205 basks in the rich autumn sun at Sayre, Pennsylvania, on October 3, 1975. Although it shares a stylistic resemblance with Raymond Loewy's T1 Duplex, the shark-nose design was the work of Hadley, Ryder & Pedersen. This carbody style was used on several different models, the RF16 being the most common.
Photo by Bill Dechau, Doug Eisele collection

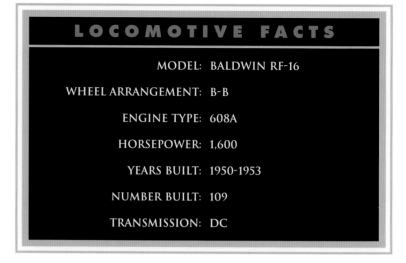

BALDWIN SHARKS

Baldwin's short, unhappy diesel building career was a sad final chapter in the company's 125-year history as America's most prolific locomotive producer. As the oldest and largest steam locomotive manufacturer, Baldwin remained firmly committed to steam technology well after it became obvious to many in the railroad industry that the diesel-electric was the way forward. Baldwin developed a practical diesel-electric switcher in the 1930s—which proved to be one of its few reliable designs—but it hesitated to develop a heavy mainline locomotive until the mid-1940s. Meanwhile, Baldwin's diesel building competitor, Electro-Motive, had introduced its successful passenger E-units in the late 1930s and its highly successful FT road freight locomotives on the eve of World War II (see page 56), giving EMD a distinct advantage in the diesel market. During the war, the high demand for electrical materials and diesel engines for military applications resulted in severe War Production Board limitations on diesel production. In many situations, the WPB encouraged railroads to order steam

locomotives when they would have preferred diesel power. During the height of the war, Baldwin earned handsome profits from the construction of hundreds of new locomotives for domestic use and export, while building some diesel switchers. The WPB permitted Baldwin to undertake diesel research, but the company failed to take full advantage of this opportunity. Its early road diesels were largely based on contemporary heavy electric locomotive designs.

Following the war, Baldwin entered the road locomotive market with a bizarre-looking multiple-engine, articulated multi-axle beast known popularly as a "Centipede." This curious locomotive was not a practical machine for many railroads, and it didn't sell well. Changing its course again, Baldwin set out to mimic Electro-Motive's successful F-unit, and in 1948 it delivered a full carbody

▲ The PRR had the largest fleet of Baldwin shark-nose diesels, which included all three models. On July 11, 1958, crews service a set of DR-4-4-15s at Kinsman Yard in Cleveland, Ohio. *Richard Jay Solomon*

▸ Mixed in with New York Central's vast fleet of Alco and Electro-Motive cab units were a handful of Baldwin sharks. An A-B set of RF16 Sharks in Central's lightning-stripe paint rolls through Sandusky, Ohio, in June 1954. The lead locomotive was renumbered 1207 and was later sold to the Monongahela Railway. *J. R. Quinn collection*

locomotive that rode on two-axle trucks, Model DR-4-4-1500 cab units. They were powered by Baldwin's 608SC diesel engine and used Westinghouse electrical gear. Baldwin's early road diesels featured a streamlining treatment similar to EMD's E- and F-units, a fact that didn't please everyone at Baldwin. According to John Kirkland, Baldwin hired the design firm Hadley, Ryder & Pedersen to develop a distinctive carbody design that would distinguish Baldwin locomotives from those of its competition, especially EMD. What the firm came up with was the famous "shark-nose" carbody, a design that bore a striking resemblance to Raymond Loewy's treatment of Pennsylvania's T1 Duplex streamliner (see page 50).

The first order of diesels to receive the new carbody design was a fleet of A1A passenger diesels for Baldwin's biggest domestic customer, the Pennsylvania Railroad. These DR-6-4-2000 "passenger sharks" were delivered in 1948. For its freight service, PRR ordered a sizable fleet of DR-4-4-1500 four-motor units, in the new carbody, later that same year.

One of the factors attributed to Baldwin's failure as a diesel locomotive manufacturer was its approaching the diesel locomotive business in the same way that it had steam. Where Electro-Motive mass-produced standard locomotive types, Baldwin tried to cater to each railroad's specific requirements. By the late 1940s, Baldwin was starting to catch on, and it built a four-unit DR-4-4-1500 shark-nose demonstrator set, in order to convince railroads to purchase its locomotives. Baldwin's colorfully painted shark-nose demo paraded around the country, testing on a variety of different lines from the tiny Lehigh & Hudson River Railroad, to big lines such as New York Central and Southern Pacific.

Baldwin's pre-1950 diesel terminology was cumbersome but logical—DR stood for diesel road locomotive; 4-4 indicated four axles and four motors; 1500 reflected the locomotive's maximum horsepower. In 1950, Baldwin upgraded its locomotive line, boosting the standard power rating of its road diesels from 1,500 horsepower to 1,600 horsepower, while simultaneously simplifying its designation system. The new sharks were thus designed as RF16 for road freight, 1,600 horsepower. The Baltimore & Ohio placed three orders for RF16s, and the New York Central also ordered a fleet of them. The Pennsylvania Railroad, always Baldwin's most loyal customer, ordered RF16s to augment its DR-4-4-1500 fleet. Probably the most obscure operators of Baldwin sharks were steel roads, Elgin, Joliet & Eastern and its sister operation, Duluth, Missabe & Iron Range. The EJ&E picked up the Baldwin demonstrator set, which it operated for a few years on its Chicago Outer Belt route, before transferring it to the DM&IR operation in northern Minnesota. This four-shark set was ultimately sold to the B&O, where it joined the railroad's RF16 fleet.

The B&O and the PRR based their RF16/DR-4-4-1500 sharks in coal and ore country, where the Baldwin four-cycle diesel could do its best work. B&O's sharks could be found working coal drags out of Benwood and Grafton, West Virginia. While PRR's sharks worked in heavy service everywhere from Enola, Pennsylvania, to Crestline, Ohio, some were assigned to Renovo, Pennsylvania, a remote Appalachian terminal on PRR's Buffalo Line. New York Central's sharks were initially based at Dewitt Yard in Syracuse, New York, right in the heart of Alco country, but they were later transferred to its lines in Ohio.

By 1956, Baldwin recognized that it was unable to compete in the diesel market and ceased its domestic locomotive production. After its demise, Baldwin's diesels soldiered on for a number of years as orphans in a world dominated by EMD. The advent of new second-generation power from EMD, General Electric, and Alco doomed oddball locomotives from the steam-diesel transition period, and in the mid-1960s, most sharks were purged from active duty and sent for scrap. In 1967, seven of New York Central's sharks escaped scrapping, and found work on the Monongahela Railway, a western Pennsylvania coal hauler. Here they toiled in relative obscurity until the early 1970s, when they were again displaced by more modern diesels. The Delaware & Hudson picked up two of Monongahela's sharks and cleaned them up, applying its flashy blue and silver paint. For a few years the last remaining pair of RF16 sharks operated in a variety of freight duties on the D&H. This tenure was short, and by 1977 they had been sold again. They ended up on the Baldwin-friendly Escanaba & Lake Superior, a line in upper Michigan where they have remained for many years, albeit no longer in working order.

During their brief career with the Delaware & Hudson, the two Baldwin sharks were often assigned to a transfer run from Binghamton, New York, over a Lehigh Valley branch to the latter's yard at Sayre, Pennsylvania. Working this transfer run, the RF16 sharks are seen at Sayre Yard alongside Lehigh Valley RS-2 No. 214. *Photo by Bill Dechau, Doug Eisele collection*

The first locomotives to receive the shark-nose carbody were Pennsylvania Railroad's six-axle, four-motor passenger locomotives, Baldwin model DR-6-4-2000. These were Baldwin's answer to EMD's successful E-unit. On May 10, 1959, exactly 90 years after the first Transcontinental Railroad was completed at Promontory, Utah, Pennsylvania's 5770 rests at Meadows Yard in New Jersey. *Richard Jay Solomon*

ALCO PA

In July 1964, four years after the Erie-Lackawanna merger, a former Erie Railroad PA is still wearing its original Erie paint and working on a suburban passenger train. The PA was a fairly unusual model on the Erie-Lackawanna, as the railroad had just 13 of them. In later years E-L's PAs worked freight trains to Chicago; in the end, all of them were retired. Richard Jay Solomon

The handsome lines of the Alco PA make it a popular diesel among enthusiasts. Delaware & Hudson PA1 No. 18 was photographed in the afternoon sun at Watervliet, New York, on August 29, 1976. The Delaware & Hudson acquired four PAs from the Santa Fe in 1967. The D&H retained the basic elements of Santa Fe's warbonnet paint scheme, substituting blue for red. *Photo by Bill Dechau, Doug Eisele collection*

▲ A resplendent Delaware & Hudson No. 16 leads Amtrak's southbound *Adirondack* at Saratoga Springs, New York. While D&H often assigned its fleet of PAs to this Amtrak run, it used them for other purposes too, including freight on occasion. D&H No. 16 was built in 1948 for the Santa Fe, working as No. 59L. *Photo by Bill Dechau, Doug Eisele collection*

ALCO PA

Although often deemed the best-looking diesel ever built, the Alco PA was neither one of the best-performing, nor one of the more numerous diesels. Still, its well-balanced design, handsome lines, 6-foot long nose, and distinctive sound have made it very popular with railway enthusiasts and it remains one of the best remembered designs of the postwar period.

In the 1940s, Alco was a premier American locomotive builder. It had been responsible for building some of the best steam locomotives of the modern era, including New York Central's Hudsons, Mohawks, and Niagaras; Union Pacific's magnificent 800 series Northerns, both its Challengers and the mammoth Big Boys; and Milwaukee Road's fast Atlantics for its high-speed Hiawathas. Of the three big steam builders, Alco had the most experience with diesel-electrics, having introduced a line of switchers, road switchers, and road locomotives before World War II. During the war, Alco and the other steam builders were largely limited by the War Production Board to the production of steam locomotives and switchers, while General Motors' Electro-Motive Division was limited to the production of road diesels. Alco's postwar strategy was to promote both steam and diesel-electric designs. Its entry in the passenger road diesel market was its 2,000 PA/PB, a powerful, streamlined machine designed to compete with EMD's already successful E-unit. The PA is the model designation for the cab locomotive, while PB is the designation for the cabless booster locomotive. Initially Alco did not use the PA/PB designations, instead describing the locomotives by their specification numbers: DL-304 for the PA, and DL-305 for the PB.

Like most Alco locomotives in the immediate postwar period, the PA/PBs used General Electric electrical equipment. They carried an Alco/GE builder plate, reflecting the close relationship between the two companies. Alco and GE had been building locomotives together since the early days of the first electrics. They had worked together on such famous machines as New York Central's S-motors and, with partner Ingersoll-Rand, built the first successful commercial diesel-electric, Central Railroad of New Jersey 1000, in 1925.

In some respects, the Alco PA was very similar to the EMD E-unit. Both locomotives were designed for passenger service, using a pair of A1A trucks (three-axle bogie trucks with two outside powered axles and an unpowered center axle for weight distribution) and featuring handsomely streamlined full-body carbodies. The PA's streamlining was more angular than the rounded "Bull Dog" front end employed on postwar E-units. Internally the PAs were very different from the E. The E-unit used a pair of 900-horsepower 567 engines—Electro-Motive's classic two-cycle diesel—to generate 1,800 horsepower; the PA employed a single

LOCOMOTIVE FACTS

MODEL:	ALCO PA
WHEEL ARRANGEMENT:	A1A-A1A
ENGINE TYPE:	16-244
HORSEPOWER:	2,000
YEARS BUILT:	1946-1949
NUMBER BUILT:	167
TRANSMISSION:	DC

turbocharged 244 engine—a four-cycle diesel introduced in 1944—to generate 2,000 horsepower. Later PAs that carried the model designation PA-2/PB-2 were more powerful and rated at 2,250 horsepower. The PA's greater horsepower and its strong lugging four-cycle engine made it a popular choice with several heavily graded railroads. Southern Pacific, known for its rugged lines, owned the largest fleet of PAs. However, the 244 engine was troublesome, making the PAs less reliable than the EMD E-unit. This resulted in lower sales, and shorter service lives. While Alco sold a total of 297 PA/PB models to 16 different American lines, this could not compare with the more than 1,200 E-units sold among many more railroads.

Initially PAs were assigned to premier passenger runs, and adorned in the most colorful liveries. Southern Pacific had them painted in its famous Daylight paint, a stunning orange, red, and sliver scheme introduced in the 1930s on its streamlined 4-8-4s. SP typically assigned PAs to the Overland Limited, City of San Francisco, and Cascade, using them primarily on its routes north and east of the company's headquarters in San Francisco. Santa Fe, which operated one of largest and longest-lived PA fleets, treated them to its colorful "warbonnet" livery, a red and silver body with black and yellow accent stripes. In later years, Santa Fe was renowned for operating large numbers of PAs on its mail trains, sometimes assigning as many as eight to one run. In the east, Lehigh Valley's maroon, black, and yellow PAs

hauled its Black Diamond and Maple Leaf, while the New Haven's sharply adorned dark green and cream PAs raced up and down its Shoreline Route between Boston and New Haven, augmenting its fleet of pre-war Alco DL109s—the largest in the nation.

Although some PA fleets received lots of attention from photographers, others went practically unnoticed. Photos of Southern Railway's PAs are particularly unusual, and on the much-photographed Pennsylvania Railroad, its small PA fleet was relatively elusive.

During the 1950s, passenger service declined rapidly, and some railroads regeared and reassigned their PAs for freight service. By the mid-1960s, most PAs had been retired, with those on Southern Pacific, Santa Fe, and Erie-Lackawanna surviving the longest. The last and most famous PAs were four former Santa Fe units, acquired by Delaware & Hudson in the late 1960s, just as most other PA owners were sending theirs for scrap. D&H painted its PAs in an attractive blue and silver variation of Santa Fe's warbonnet. For several years in the mid-1970s these locomotives were regularly used to haul Amtrak's *Adirondack* over D&H rails from the Albany area to Montreal, Quebec. D&H sent its PAs to Morrison-Knudsen for rebuilding in the late 1970s, then lent them to Boston's Massachusetts Bay Transportation Authority (MBTA) for a stint in suburban service, before shipping them to Mexico. While the last PA fleet survived south of the border, it suffered from wrecks and neglect. In 2000, two PAs were repatriated and are now awaiting restoration in Oregon.

New Haven's *Yankee Clipper* races through Canton Junction, Massachusetts, behind a pair of PAs on January 31, 1954. New Haven's PAs were delivered in its attractive dark green and cream paint with the traditional script herald on the nose. This scheme would eventually give way to the more modern, geometric red, white, and black. *George C. Corey*

Workmen place a plaque that reads "Freedom Train Locomotive" on an Alco PA. This locomotive hauled the Freedom Train on its 37,000-mile nationwide tour from September 17, 1947, to January 22, 1949, before going into service on the Gulf, Mobile and Ohio Railroad. It was the first locomotive to operate in all 48 states. *Courtesy Bob's Photos*

ELECTRO-MOTIVE GP9

A bright candy-apple red Soo Line GP9 rests at the old Milwaukee Road Pig's Eye Yard in January 1994.
More than 40 years after the GP9 debuted, many of them were still hard at work on American railroads.
Brian Solomon

Electro-Motive GP9

The phenomenal success of Electro-Motive's GP9 was demonstrated by the great number produced and the locomotive's exceptional longevity in tough operating conditions. More than 4,200 GP9s were built for service in North America over a 10-year period from 1953 to 1963, making them the single most numerous diesel-electric model in the Western world. There were more GP9s built than all Baldwin diesel models put together. Although the GP9 is more than 40 years old, quite a few still soldier on, some of them having been rebuilt several times.

In Electro-Motive lexicon, the initials "GP" stood for "general purpose," and the locomotives are often called "jeeps" as a result, though the name has nothing to do with the popular four-wheel-drive vehicle of the same name. The connotation of adaptability associated with an all-terrain vehicle must have pleased EMD. The GP was not known for its striking looks; in fact, even the locomotive's designer, Electro-Motive's Dick Dilworth, called it ugly. But looks were not an issue. It wasn't the GP's aesthetic attributes that made the locomotive a winner; it was its power, reliability, and versatility.

Electro-Motive had been reluctant to adopt the road switcher type, which its competitors had been quick to embrace. In 1941, Alco had originated the road switcher type with its Model RS-1 (see RS-3, page 66). By 1946 Alco, Baldwin, and Fairbanks-Morse were mass-producing road switchers. Initially these efforts didn't concern GM, which was selling as many F, E, and switcher models as it could build. Its raw success marketing standard types had totally overshadowed the efforts of its competitors.

After the war, EMD dabbled in building road switcher-like locomotives, such as the NW5 in 1946 and the BL1/BL2 in 1947, but these models didn't sell well compared to the standard models. EMD's NW5 shared attributes with Alco's successful RS-1 light road switcher, but EMD only sold 13 units in North America. The BL1/BL2 was something of a hybrid F-unit with some road switcher qualities. While admired by enthusiasts, EMD sold just 59 units. Both of these attempts were just anomalies in EMD's North American production.

Initially the "covered wagon" style of road diesel was favored by railroads, and each of the large builders had its own line: EMD with its E and F; Alco its PA and FA; Baldwin with "Sharks," "Centipedes," and baby-faced "Gravel girdies"; and Fairbanks-Morse with "Erie builts" and C-liners. There were valid reasons for this preference. Diesels had become associated with the popular streamliners of the mid-1930s, and the public expected new diesels to have a flashy, streamlined appearance. The new look helped sell diesels. Carbody diesels matched nicely with the new streamlined trains, and the overall aesthetic was visually pleasing. There was another side to the need for a carbody that was often neglected in period promotional materials. Early diesels were subject to regular failures, despite their glowing performance statistics and clever publicity stunts. Road failures were among the reasons early diesel sets typically consisted of two or more "units," and some types, such as the EMD E-unit, had two engines for power. If one engine failed, the others could keep pulling, while it was repaired. Some repairs were

Over the years, two of Canadian National's United States subsidiaries, Central Vermont and Grand Trunk Western, intermingled their fleets of GP9s. On July 13, 1988, four GP9s lead the southbound 447 across the high bridge over the Millers River at Millers Falls, Massachusetts. The lead locomotive wears Grand Trunk blue and orange paint, while the others are in CV's green and gold.
Brian Solomon

made in the comfort of a shop, but it was common for mechanics to ride along with the locomotive crew in order to make major repairs while the locomotives were traveling at speed. There are numerous tales of Electro-Motive mechanics changing out broken cylinders and rods on the earlier Es and FTs on the roll. This is where the car-body came in. It provided protection to the men working on the locomotive as it raced along.

Another consideration in cab-unit consists was overcoming the resistance to dieselization by labor unions. Initially some unions insisted that each and every diesel locomotive be manned in the same way that steam locomotives had been. Obviously paying a crew for each locomotive would have nullified much of the savings that railroads hoped to achieve by using diesels instead of steam, especially considering that multiple-unit technology permitted one engineer to control many diesels. One way the railroads overcame this conflict was by declaring that a four-unit A-B-B-A diesel set was one locomotive, and not four separate locomotives. Often these early sets were numbered accordingly. For example, F-unit sets used letter suffixes after the number to distinguish the different units. The whole concept of a B-unit "booster" engine was designed to avoid union problems, and save the cost of a cab on each diesel.

By the late 1940s, the diesel had been sold to the railroads and there was no turning back. Flashy streamlining was no longer needed to convince railroad managers that they needed diesel power, as the performance figures demonstrated the diesel's capabilities. After more than a decade of mass-producing diesel engines and locomotives, EMD had dramatically improved its reliability

LOCOMOTIVE FACTS

MODEL:	EMD GP9
WHEEL ARRANGEMENT:	B-B
ENGINE TYPE:	16-567C
HORSEPOWER:	1,750
YEARS BUILT:	1954-1963
NUMBER BUILT:	4,092
TRANSMISSION:	DC

and performance. Locomotives rarely failed on the road, and it was no longer necessary to send mechanics and riders along with diesel sets. For the most part, the labor issues had been smoothed over, and railroads were not required to have a man in each locomotive. (Yet most lines were still required to employ firemen for another couple of decades, despite the obvious lack of fire.)

These changes in the diesel market encouraged EMD to develop its own road switcher type. In 1949, Electro-Motive Division debuted its first true road switcher, a 1,500-horsepower hood unit powered by EMD's successful 567B engine, designated Model GP7. The road switcher had several advantages over carbody-style locomotives. Road switchers were cheaper to build, provided easier access for maintenance, and had numerous operating advantages. They were bidirectional—thus didn't require elaborate turning facilities—and could handle many different duties, from switching to passenger trains, and even heavy freight. The GP's versatility was consistent with an industry trend toward universal locomotive designs, rather than more specialized machines.

The GP7 used most of the same components as EMD's E and F, and was introduced along with the F7 as part of EMD's latest line of locomotives. The GP7 sold extremely well, outpacing all other models, even EMD's other popular types. In 1953, EMD replaced the GP7, with the slightly more powerful, and even more reliable GP9, rated at 1,750 horsepower. These GPs complemented existing

EMD fleets nicely, as they could be easily operated in multiples with existing EMD types. By the mid-1950s, it was common to see Fs and GPs lashed together on long freights. Most railroads ordered GP9s with operator cabs, which allowed the railroads greater flexibility in assigning locomotives. The "building block" principle was used when assigning locomotives to trains, particularly heavy freights: if more power was needed, another locomotive could be easily added without concern for whether it was an A- or a B-unit, or if its cab was facing the right direction. If a locomotive was needed to switch a yard or a branch line, one could be set out as needed, because the GPs were equally suited to road, branch, and yard operation. The Union Pacific and the Pennsylvania Railroad still saw cost advantages to cabless "B" units, and ordered cabless GP9Bs to augment their fleets.

In many ways, the GP9 was the perfect locomotive, and it arrived on the scene just in time to allow many lines to complete their dieselization programs. When a new fleet of GP9s arrived on the property, railroads sent their last steam locomotives into storage, or directly to scrap. Some lines, such as the Boston & Maine, traded in older EMDs for GP9s. It may seem odd that as early as the mid-1950s a railroad was already trading in diesels, but by that time B&M's brown and maroon World War II vintage FTs had turned many miles for the railroad. More than 40 years later, a few of the old GPs that replaced the FTs are still running—testimony to the GP's solid design.

GENERAL ELECTRIC U25B

Maine Central U25B No. 238 is seen at East Deerfield, Massachusetts, on August 30, 1987. The U25B can usually be identified by a longer nose section than was used by most other General Electric U-series locomotives, and by a characteristic step-up section of the gangway toward the rear of the carbody. A few early U28Bs also had these features.
Brian Solomon

Erie-Lackawanna U25Bs lead an afternoon westbound freight through Smithboro, New York, on October 27, 1975. Erie-Lackawanna had a fleet of 27 U25Bs built in 1964 and 1965. The old Erie Railroad mainline between Binghamton and Hornell, New York, saw heavy freight traffic under Erie-Lackawanna ownership. *Photo by Bill Dechau, Doug Eisele collection*

General Electric U25B

Until 1953, Alco diesel-electric locomotives proudly displayed Alco-GE builder's plates, which symbolized the longtime partnership between the two companies. General Electric and the Alco component Schenectady Locomotive Works teamed up in the 1890s to build straight electric locomotives. (Alco was formed in 1901 from the merger of a number of independent steam locomotive builders.) The two companies had worked together on many projects, including such significant locomotives as New York Central's pioneering T-motors (see pages 134–137), and the very first diesel-electric boxcabs, built in the 1920s along with engine maker Ingersoll-Rand. When Alco formally entered the diesel locomotive market, General Electric was its natural partner for supplying electrical components. By the early 1950s, Alco had lost considerable market share to General Motors' Electro-Motive Division, and there were complaints in the industry regarding the quality of Alco's locomotives. This displeased General Electric, which broke with Alco and quietly began developing its own line of road diesels.

By the time it dissolved its relationship with Alco, General Electric was well established as a locomotive producer, although it did not have its own road diesel line at that time. GE had built steam-electric and gas-electric turbines for Union Pacific, straight electrics for a variety of roads, and even had its own line of diesel-electric switchers using small Cooper-Bessemer diesel engines, which were popular for branch line and yard work. In 1954, GE built a four-unit experimental diesel-electric, using 8-cylinder and 12-cylinder Cooper-Bessemer engines. For these experimentals, GE used a car-body style similar to that found on the Alco-GE FA cab units and

▲ Erie-Lackawanna No. 2527 leads an eastbound train through the Canisteo River Valley, east of Adrian, New York, in October 1975. The scenic splendor of this remote valley, with its sweeping curves and high shale cliffs, has long been a favorite place for photographers to capture trains in action. *Photo by Bill Dechau, Doug Eisele collection*

◄ Maine Central U25B No. 238 at East Deerfield, Massachusetts, on August 30, 1987. *Brian Solomon*

In April 1968, a Rock Island U25B leads a GP35 and two Southern Pacific SD45s through Blue Island, Illinois. General Electric entered the heavy diesel-electric locomotive market with its U25B in 1960. In its day, the 2,500-horsepower U25B was considered a high-horsepower road locomotive. *Richard Jay Solomon*

GE's E2b straight electrics built for the Pennsylvania Railroad. While this style is closely associated with Alco products, GE had actually done the exterior carbody styling. In 1956, following thousands of miles of prototype testing, GE introduced an 1,800-horsepower road switcher diesel for the export market, a move that brought GE one step closer to entering the domestic market.

By the late 1950s domestic sales of new locomotives were poor. Many railroads had completed their dieselization ahead of schedule and there was not much need for more locomotives, following the production boom of the postwar years. Baldwin and Fairbanks-Morse, the two weakest diesel builders, had exited the market because of their inability to compete with Electro-Motive. This had left Alco as the only other major builder after EMD. General Electric recognized the cyclical nature of the locomotive business. The postwar boom had subsided, but when locomotives bought during that time wore out, there would be a renewed buying frenzy.

Another consideration in GE's timing to enter the diesel market was the lack of domestic interest in alternatives to diesel-electric locomotive technology, which General Electric had supported—specifically, the implementation of overhead electrification and gas turbine technology. By the mid-1950s, the diesel-electric had prevailed over all other forms of railroad motive power in the United States. While there was still occasional interest in electrification schemes, the bulk of the locomotive business was diesel.

GE had the talent and the finances to effect a practical long-term strategy toward locomotive development. The company was large and diverse enough to carry on research and development for years, before needing to sell locomotives. Thus it waited out the lean years, while perfecting its designs, and then jumped into the market when sales began to pick up.

In the late 1950s, GE expanded and refined the Cooper-Bessemer diesel design, creating a high-horsepower, four-cycle, 16-cylinder

engine designated the FDL16. In 1959 GE built a pair of test locomotives, designated XP24, using the FDL16. This engine generated 2,400 horsepower, significantly more power than most commercial diesel-electrics on the road at that time. Then in 1960, GE surprised the industry when it boosted the output of the FDL16 to 2,500 horsepower and debuted domestic test locomotives designated U25B. These became demonstrators for its domestic "Universal" line. Once GE was certain that it had a good product, it went all out and built no less than four sets of demonstrators and embarked on a nationwide advertising campaign to sell them to the railroads.

The U25B designation for GE's new locomotive is simple to decipher: "U" for Universal, "25" for 2,500 horsepower, and "B" for four-axle trucks. For more than a dozen years GE's designations would follow this basic system. The U25B's high-horsepower road switcher configuration was a function of the times. Just 10 years earlier, most railroads were buying full carbody-style locomotives. But by the mid-1950s this once-common style had fallen out of favor, and

LOCOMOTIVE FACTS

MODEL: GENERAL ELECTRIC U25B

WHEEL ARRANGEMENT: B-B

ENGINE TYPE: 7FDL-16

HORSEPOWER: 2,500

YEARS BUILT: 1959-1966

NUMBER BUILT: 476

TRANSMISSION: DC

the boxy, utilitarian road switcher represented the bulk of locomotive sales. Another change occurred just as GE was beginning to sell locomotives. This was the advent of the low short-hood, which became a standard option on most road switchers in the 1960s. The low short-hood provided operating crews with better forward visibility. The first U25Bs were built with high short-hoods, giving them an outward appearance similar to Fairbanks-Morse's road switchers. Later U25Bs featured a low short-hood, which became the standard format for GE diesels. Despite the predominance of the low short-hood on American locomotives built after 1960, some lines, such as the Norfolk & Western, continued to order locomotives with high short-hoods.

Union Pacific, which had a reputation for powerful locomotives, was the first road to sample the U25B. It had operated some of the largest steam locomotives in the United States; was the only line to opt for a fleet of gas turbine locomotives known for their high output; and had recently experimented with its own coal-fired gas turbine. Dissatisfied with the basic GP9, UP had boosted the power of this locomotive by adding a turbocharger. It also was a large buyer of EMD's own turbocharged SD24 model. While interested in the promise of the U25B, it bought only 16 of them. By contrast, Southern Pacific, also on a quest for more power, acquired a fleet of 68 U25Bs and went on to amass a substantial fleet of GE diesels. The largest single buyer of U25Bs was New York Central, which acquired 70 of them.

The U25B was designed as a heavy road locomotive, and typically operated in multiples, usually in sets of three or four. For the most part, they were used to haul mainline freight. Between 1959 and 1966, General Electric built a total of 478 U25Bs, and between 1963 and 1965 it built 113 U25Cs, the six-axle cousin to the U25B.

While these totals are small compared to the vast numbers of EMD GP30s and GP35s sold during the same period, they represented a significant market share of new locomotives—a remarkable achievement for a company that had just entered the new road diesel business. Many railroads traded in older diesel models to GE on orders for new U25s, thus thinning the ranks of Baldwins and older Alcos. Many of these locomotives were just 10 years old, having been used to replace steam. For this reason, the U25B is considered a second-generation diesel—that is, a diesel that replaced the first generation of diesel models.

The U25B firmly established GE's place as a new diesel locomotive builder, and it was succeeded by a long line of improved models. The original U25Bs had relatively short careers, however, compared to the EMD and even Alco road units built at the same time. By the mid-1970s, U25Bs were ripe for retirement and trade-in. Most of GE's U25B production was scrapped during the late 1970s, and by the early 1980s there were very few U25Bs left running on American rails. In contrast, numerous EMD GP30s and GP35s soldiered on, and many were modified and rebuilt. In 1975, Southern Pacific rebuilt one U25B in an experiment to extend the life of the locomotive; later in 1977, SP contracted Morrison-Knudsen to rebuild four of its U25Bs with Sulzer engines. Neither effort had a long-term impact on the service life of SP's U25 fleet. One of the last fleets of U25Bs comprised 14 former Rock Island locomotives bought by the Maine Central in 1980, after the Rock folded. These survived for almost another decade, long after most U25s had vanished from the scene.

▲ In 1963 General Electric introduced a six-motor road locomotive, the 2,500-horsepower U25C. This model didn't sell as well as its pioneering U25B—just 113 units, compared to the U25B's 478. Later GE six-motor units would fair much better, and today six-motor locomotives represent the majority of General Electric's domestic production. On April 6, 1976, a former Penn Central U25C leads an eastbound freight at Bison Yard, in Buffalo, New York. *Photo by Bill Dechau, Doug Eisele collection*

◄ Maine Central U25B 229 at the Boston & Maine's Lowell, Massachusetts, yard in the spring of 1987. Maine Central acquired 14 former Rock Island U25Bs following Rock's liquidation in 1980, including this one built new for the Rock in 1965. *Brian Solomon*

ELECTRO-MOTIVE GP40

A pair of Wisconsin Central GP40s are lettered for The Campaign Train for Science, *with the* Laird Express *in the WC logo. They hauled a special promotional passenger train on May 2, 1996. While a few specially built GP40s were used as passenger locomotives, the vast majority of the GP40 production line operated in freight service.* Brian Solomon

Guilford Rail System GP40s loom ominously in the morning mist at East Deerfield, Massachusetts, on September 6, 2000. Today, the large railroads rely on modern six-motor safety cab locomotives to haul most freight. The day of the high-horsepower four-axle locomotive has come and gone, yet a few railroads still cling to secondhand GP40s to move trains.
Brian Solomon

Five Rochester & Southern GP40s lead the overnight RS freight southbound at Caledonia, New York, on February 18, 1988. Two years earlier, the R&S acquired several former New York Central GP40s from Conrail for its mainline operations and took over the former Buffalo, Rochester & Pittsburgh Fourth Subdivision (Rochester to Ashford Junction) from CSX.
Brian Solomon

ELECTRO-MOTIVE GP40

The GP40's common utilitarian appearance—a boxy, all-business look shared with many different EMD models of the 1960s, 1970s, and 1980s—reveals little about the locomotive. To the untrained eye, a GP40 looks nearly identical to a variety of different models. Only close observation of its spotting features will identify it. So, one may ask, why is the GP40 significant?

The GP40 is a milestone locomotive and one of EMD's best-selling second-generation models. Its success story is often ignored because of its bland appearance and seemingly secondary status when compared to its larger cousins, the six-motor SD40 and SD45—models introduced about the same time that shared the same technological improvements.

Boston & Maine's last new locomotives were a fleet of 18 GP40-2s from Electro-Motive. Nearly new Boston & Maine No. 314 is at Rigby Yard in Portland, Maine, in 1978. While the GP40-2 was nearly identical to the GP40 externally, it had many improvements on the inside. *George S. Pitarys*

LOCOMOTIVE FACTS

MODEL: EMD GP40

WHEEL ARRANGEMENT: B-B

ENGINE TYPE: 16-645E3

HORSEPOWER: 3.000

YEARS BUILT: 1965-1971

NUMBER BUILT: 1.243

TRANSMISSION: DC

By the end of the 1950s Electro-Motive was suffering from its own success. It had won its place as America's largest locomotive producer, successfully providing thousands upon thousands of diesel-electrics in an amazingly short span of time. This facilitated the rapid demise of the steam locomotive, and in less than 15 years virtually all American railroads had converted their locomotive fleets from steam to diesel. EMD had faced competition from several builders immediately following World War II, but it outpaced them all by mass-producing high-quality locomotives, and built the lion's share of new diesel-electrics. By the late 1950s, EMD had effectively driven longtime builder Baldwin out of the locomotive

business, and relegated the once-strong Alco to a distant second position. By this time, Fairbanks-Morse, which entered the market at the end of the war, had also effectively ceased its domestic locomotive production.

Once the railroads made the conversion to diesel, EMD's domestic sales dropped off. It tried to convince railroads to trade in older models, such as its wartime FTs, for newer and more efficient designs, but with limited success. A few lines, such as the Boston & Maine, traded in their FT fleets for new GP9s, and other lines sent in older Fs for rebuilding, but new locomotive sales remained flat compared to the boom years of the late 1940s and early 1950s.

Traditionally, EMD had shunned turbocharging, preferring its normally aspirated Roots blower to provide sufficient oxygen for combustion. When Union Pacific rebuilt a number of EMD GP9s with turbochargers at its Omaha Shops, however, EMD took notice. In an effort to rekindle the market's enthusiasm for new locomotives, EMD fitted a turbocharger to its 567 prime mover.

As the 1960s dawned, the market for new locomotives evolved. But EMD's initial turbocharged models, its four-axle, four-motor GP20, and six-axle, six-motor SD24, did not sell particularly well. These locomotives were not significantly more powerful than earlier models. Rated at 2,000 horsepower, the turbocharged GP20 provided only 250 additional horsepower over the extremely popular GP9.

Complicating matters, EMD was faced with serious competition. General Electric, which had refrained from building its own line of domestic road locomotives during the steam-diesel transition period, instead choosing to partner with Alco until the early 1950s, debuted its own line of high-horsepower domestic locomotives in 1960. GE's four-motor U25B was rated at 2,500 horsepower, significantly more powerful than any comparable EMD product (see page 84). EMD reacted by further boosting the horsepower of its 567 engine, introducing the 2,250-horsepower GP30 in 1961, and the 2,500-horsepower GP35 in 1963. Both of these four-motor locomotives sold very well, but EMD had pushed the 567 engine to its effective limit. Electro-Motive's engineers had nearly doubled the output of the 567 over its 25-year history, and they realized they needed a new design.

Electro-Motive Division set out to design a whole new line of locomotives. Since the late 1930s, Electro-Motive had stressed mass-produced locomotives with interchangeable parts. While it had gradually improved its locomotive designs, introducing incremental changes with successive new models, it had retained the same

essential design parameters to avoid producing incompatible locomotives. Finally, EMD recognized that to build significantly better, more powerful locomotives, it needed to sacrifice compatibility for overall improvement. And it did so in typical EMD fashion by introducing a variety of new models simultaneously, featuring a number of significant design improvements.

One of the most significant improvements was its new diesel engine. Working from the successful 567, EMD engineers increased the cylinder bore from 8 1/2 inches to 9 1/16 inches, expanding the total displacement from 567 to 645 cubic inches. Initially the rotational speed of the 645 engine remained the same as that of the last generation, 567 to 900 revolutions per minute. The 645 also retained the same basic two-stroke diesel engine design—a quality that separated EMD from all other American locomotive manufacturers, who preferred traditional four-stroke designs. Among the other improvements were an enhanced high-capacity traction motor design that could accommodate the increase in

In October 2000, Green Mountain No. 302 leads an excursion over the New England Central Railroad at Stafford Springs, Connecticut. This passenger train, sponsored by the Eastern Connecticut Transit Alliance, operated between Willimantic, Connecticut, and Brattleboro, Vermont. Skilled locomotive engineer Steve Carlson is at the throttle. *Brian Solomon*

engine output, and a new AC-DC rectifier power transmission system (not to be confused with three-phase AC traction, which was developed much later).

In 1965, after several years of testing, EMD announced nine new locomotive models, all incorporating these significant technological improvements. The first of these new models to enter regular service was a group of GP40s ordered by the New York Central. The GP40 used a 16-cylinder turbocharged 645 engine to generate a whopping 3,000 horsepower, making it the most powerful American-made four-axle diesel locomotive. Although just 500 horsepower more powerful than General Electric's U25B, it was twice as powerful as the thousands of EMD F3s, F7s, and GP7s running on American lines, which gave railroads the incentive to replace their older locomotives at a two-for-one ratio.

The GP40 was an instant success. A high-horsepower four-axle locomotive is well suited for fast freight operations, such as intermodal services, which were enjoying rapid growth in the mid-1960s. Consists of three and four GP40s could sprint along American mainlines at 70 miles per hour with more than a mile of piggybacks (trailers on flat cars) in tow. Between 1965 and 1971, EMD produced more than 1,200 GP40s for service on lines in North America. In addition, two variations of the GP40 were developed for passenger services, the GP40P, with a steam generator, and the GP40TC, with a headed power generator—to provide heat and electrical power for passenger trains—instead of the traditional steam generator.

In 1972, EMD introduced its "Dash-2" line, which further improved on its locomotive designs. Most of these improvements did not alter the external appearance of its locomotives, but did increase their reliability. The GP40-2 was another successful seller, and served essentially the same market as the GP40. Externally, the GP40-2 was nearly identical to the GP40. A GP40-2 has a small oval sighting window below the radiator vents at the back of the locomotive that helps distinguish it from the GP40. Internally, the GP40-2 had many improvements, including a better wheel slip control system.

The success of Electro-Motive's GP40 inspired General Electric and Alco to develop their own 3,000-horsepower four-axle models. However, neither the GE U30b nor the Alco C-430 sold nearly as the well as the GP40.

The GP40 and GP40-2 can be identified from other similar appearing EMD models, such as the GP35 and the 2,000-horsepower GP38, by the exhaust fans on the roof at the rear of the carbody. Only the GP40 models have three fans in a row at the same level. The GP35 has a center fan lower than the outside two, and the GP38 models have just two fans.

MONTREAL LOCOMOTIVE WORKS
SIX-MOTOR LOCOMOTIVES

The Cape Breton & Central Nova Scotia was one of the last railways in North America to use big MLW locomotives on through freights. On July 25, 1997, CB&CNS No. 2032, Lord Byron, *named for the romantic poet, leads freight No. 305 at Sydney Mines, Nova Scotia.* Brian Solomon

4571

MONTREAL LOCOMOTIVE WORKS
SIX-MOTOR LOCOMOTIVES

Alco developed its Century line in the early 1960s to better compete with Electro-Motive Division, and Alco's one-time diesel building partner, General Electric. When GE entered the heavy locomotive market in 1960, it quickly surpassed Alco as the number two American diesel builder—a position Alco had held since the end of World War II. The Century line introduced a number of technological improvements aimed to increase reliability, and featured a new carbody style. The Century embodied a clean, modern aesthetic, yet retained a classic railroad look. It was a better-looking machine than the utilitarian, boxy locomotives offered by Electro-Motive and General Electric. Unfortunately for Alco, the new Century line did not compare well technologically to its EMD and GE rivals. The combined domestic sales of Alco's C-424 and C-425 (four-motor road switchers rated at 2,400 and 2,500 horsepower, respectively) totaled just 144 locomotives, compared to GE's 478 U25Bs (see page 84) and EMD's 1,250 GP35s.

Alco's C-430, a 3,000-horsepower road switcher, faired even worse against the competition. Between July 1966 and February 1968, Alco sold just 16 of this model. By comparison, GE sold 295 of its 3,000-horsepower U30B, while EMD took the lion's share of the market with 1,201 GP40 sales (see page 90). Alco faired a little better with its six-motor locomotives. It sold 135 C-628s domestically between 1963 and 1968, 77 C-630s between 1965 and 1967, and 34 C-636s in 1967 and 1968. In addition to its American sales, Alco sold to both Mexico and Canada, in addition to the overseas market. But compared to the huge numbers of locomotives that General Motors and General Electric were moving, Alco's totals were pitiful.

Montreal Locomotive Works (MLW) served as Alco's Canadian subsidiary from the turn of the nineteenth century until 1969, when Alco finally exited the American locomotive market. In the diesel era, MLW primarily produced Alco locomotives for Canadian Railroads. While some MLW locomotives were virtually indistinguishable from Alco models, others were distinctively Canadian. After the demise of Alco, MLW continued to build locomotives based on Alco's designs until it was acquired by Bombardier in 1979. Among

LOCOMOTIVE FACTS	
MODEL:	MLW M-636
WHEEL ARRANGEMENT:	C-C
ENGINE TYPE:	16-251E
HORSEPOWER:	3,600
YEARS BUILT:	1969-1975
NUMBER BUILT:	100
TRANSMISSION:	DC

the locomotives that MLW manufactured during this time were the M630 and M636, derived from Alco's Century-series C630 and C636 models.

Externally there were a few minor differences between the MLW M-630/M-636 and comparable Century models. The Canadian locomotives had slightly different radiator configurations, and rode on a different type of truck. Prior to Alco's exit, Montreal had also produced six-motor Century designs, and in most respects these locomotives were the same as those built at Alco's Schenectady, New York, facility. Between November 1969 and November 1973, MLW produced 75 M-630s for use in Canada and Mexico. The M-636 remained in production until 1975, and a total of 111 locomotives were built for North American service.

The M-630 and M-636 were 69 feet, 6 inches long, the same as the Alco models, and they used a 16-cylinder 251E engine. The M-630's engine worked at 1,000 rpm to produce 3,000 horsepower, while the M-636's worked at 1,100 rpm for a 3,600-horsepower output.

In the 1960s, EMD's SD45 had set the market threshold at 3,600 horsepower. While a few experimental locomotives pushed this figure higher, 3,600 horsepower seemed the practical limit for a six-motor direct current diesel-electric at this time.

By the mid-1970s, reliability problems, higher maintenance costs, and greater fuel consumption associated with the higher output of the SD45, C-636, and other locomotives led most North American railroads to settle for 3,000-horsepower models that had

▲ Alco locomotives were known for their propensity to billow black smoke. Cape Breton & Central Nova Scotia No. 2003 leads eastbound freight No. 306 upgrade at Marshy Hope in July 1997. The 2003 is a C-630M built for Canadian National by the Montreal Locomotive Works in December 1967. *Brian Solomon*

◀ Cartier Railway Alco C-636 No. 79 leads an empty ore train northward through the Sept Iles National Park north of Port Cartier, Quebec. This ore-hauling railroad is among the most remote lines in eastern Canada, traversing 260 miles of wilderness between Port Cartier on the Gulf of St. Lawrence and Mont Wright. *Brian Solomon*

99

Nova Scotia is one of Canada's best kept secrets. Its people are friendly, the scenery is sublime, and the ice cream is wonderful. It is also one of the last places where one can learn to speak Scottish Gaelic. On July 24, 1997, a Cape Breton & Central Nova Scotia freight rolls west at Cape Jack along the Gulf of St. Lawrence. *Brian Solomon*

better reliability. In 1971, however, MLW was still pushing the power threshold and manufactured a single 4,000-horsepower six-motor locomotive, Model M-640. This formidable machine used an 18-cylinder 251E engine, and weighed 390,000 pounds. It was a monster at the time, but two decades later, locomotives with a 4,000-horsepower rating (and higher) would be commonplace on North American railways. MLW sold the M-640 to Canadian Pacific. In 1986, Canadian Pacific used the locomotive as a test bed for developing a three-phase alternating current traction system.

Montreal Locomotive Works' primary market was the two large Canadian railways, the privately owned Canadian Pacific Railway (known for a while as CP Rail) and the nationally owned Canadian National Railway. In addition, MLW occasionally built locomotives for various smaller Canadian and American railways. Canadian Pacific initially purchased its M-630s with the intent to operate them in heavy mainline service in western Canada, but this area quickly became the domain of CP's SD40-2 fleet, and the MLWs spent most of their working lives on lines in the eastern provinces.

Despite their odd-ball status, the MLW six-motors had the proverbial cat's nine lives. In the late 1980s and 1990s, they seemed to be perpetually at the end of the road. At times the remaining fleet would be sent into storage, only to be retrieved again and again for new assignments. A few roamed on former Delaware & Hudson routes after CP acquired that property in 1990, so for a time they were regular visitors in New York and

MLW six-motor fleet, but some of these found second careers on other Canadian lines. Almost a dozen former MLW-built C-630s, and a single M-636, were acquired by the Cape Breton & Central Nova Scotia Railway in the mid-1990s.

The CB&CNS was created as the result of CN's desire to spin off lightly used feeder lines. Initially the CB&CNS was part of the RailTex family of short lines, and is now part of Rail America, a large short-line operator that acquired RailTex in 1999. The CB&CNS runs from Truro in western Nova Scotia to Sydney in the east, and has a few short branches. Until 1998, this railroad was one of the final strongholds for big MLW locomotives, and they were regularly assigned to daily through freights. Most were painted in CB&CNS's attractive black and yellow paint scheme, with a large red lion to reflect the region's Scottish heritage. Many were named after literary and political figures, such as Lord Byron, Sir Arthur Conan Doyle, and Sir Walter Scott.

By 2001, the last large fleet of Alco/MLW six-motor locomotives served the ore-hauling Cartier Railway, which operates 260 miles of railroad between Port Cartier, Quebec, and Mont Wright. This is an isolated railroad that was built in the 1950s specifically as an ore conveyor. Depending on mine output, the Cartier can move up to five heavily laden ore trains every 24 hours. Its fleet of C-636/M-636 diesels is a mix of new and used locomotives. A few were acquired directly from the manufacturers, while the remainder were picked up secondhand.

The Cartier Railway traverses largely uninhabited territory, some of which lies in the Sept Iles National Park. Long sections of the railway are completely inaccessible by paved road, forcing the company to transport crews by helicopter. The day of the six-motor 251 is nearly done, as the Cartier is about to acquire a new fleet. As of winter 2001, new General Electric locomotives were on order. It is expected that a few of the older locomotives will be retained for support work after the GEs arrive. Several American short lines have also acquired MLW six-motor locomotives secondhand, and these will likely survive for a while longer.

Considering their comparatively poor sales, the Alco/MLW six-motor locomotives had remarkable life spans in heavy service. Their handsome appearance, scarce numbers, and distinctive powerful sound has long made them a popular quarry for railroad enthusiasts and photographers.

◄ Cape Breton & Central Nova Scotia C-630M No. 2029 catches the setting sun at Afton, Nova Scotia. *Brian Solomon*

▼ The Cartier Railway's crews are treated to the scenery of the Sept Iles National Park, where they are likely to see moose and other woodland creatures. A southbound ore train passes ilepost 36 with M-636 No. 82 in the lead. This is one of several locomotives Cartier bought new from MLW. *Brian Solomon*

ELECTRO-MOTIVE TUNNEL MOTORS

A trio of Rio Grande SD40T-2s lead a westbound freight at Byers Canyon, Colorado, in September 1989. The Southern Pacific and Rio Grande were the only two railroads to buy this model new from EMD. It seems fitting that in the late 1980s the two companies came under a common management. Brian Solomon

LOCOMOTIVE FACTS

MODEL: EMD SD45T-2

WHEEL ARRANGEMENT: C-C

ENGINE TYPE: 16-645E

HORSEPOWER: 3,600

YEARS BUILT: 1972-1975

NUMBER BUILT: 247

TRANSMISSION: DC

▲ Southern Pacific SD45T-2 6794 is in full dynamic as it rolls through Eder, California, on the tail end of a long freight, descending the east slope of Donner Pass. Southern Pacific rebuilt and repainted many of its six-motor locomotives in the 1980s. Strict California environmental laws forced SP to use substandard paint, however, and after just a few years, many repainted locomotives were fading badly.
Brian Solomon

▶ On May 30, 1992, a westbound Southern Pacific freight crawls out of tunnel 41 at Donner Summit, as a cloud of exhaust smoke pours forth from the 2-mile-long bore. This is precisely the situation for which the Tunnel Motor was intended, to help the big locomotive's air intake when operating in long tunnels at high altitudes.
Brian Solomon

ELECTRO-MOTIVE TUNNEL MOTORS

High in the California Sierra, a quintet of Southern Pacific diesels shatter the serenity of the mountain solitude as they claw their way toward Donner Pass with 4,440 tons in tow. This is no ordinary route, and these are no ordinary machines. Donner Pass is one of the oldest and certainly one of the most difficult mountain crossings in the American West. It was surveyed in the early 1860s by railroad visionary Theodore Judah as part of the original Transcontinental Railroad—America's most famous line, completed at Promontory, Utah, in May 1869. Donner Pass is particularly difficult, because it crosses the spine of the Sierra Nevada, forcing the tracks to rise from just above sea level at the base of the grade near Roseville, California, to an elevation of just over 7,000 feet above sea level at Donner Summit, in roughly 90 miles. This is one of the longest continuous climbs in the United States. It combines notoriously steep grades (reaching a maximum of 2.4 percent), tight curves, high altitudes, and numerous tunnels and snowsheds. In the winter Donner sees extremely heavy snowfall, known to exceed 800 inches in a single season. This mandates the use of snowsheds at key locations. At one time much of the railroad from Emigrant Gap to Andover, a distance of roughly 30 miles, was covered by sheds.

In the steam era, the difficult Donner crossing resulted in a distinctive American steam locomotive design, SP's massive cab-ahead (or cab-forward) articulateds. These were specially designed for snowshed territory, where the exhaust gases from the big locomotives threatened to asphyxiate crews.

In the diesel era, Donner Pass resulted in another distinctive locomotive, Electro-Motive's "Tunnel Motor," SD45T-2 and SD40T-2.

Steam locomotives were usually designed for a specific segment of railroad operation. This practice resulted in each railroad having a unique fleet of locomotives, often custom designed by the manufacturers. The advent of the mass-produced diesel-electric ended this trend. Instead, manufacturers offered a selection of different types to all railroads. The primary differences between one fleet and another were found in relatively minor accessories, such as headlights, horns, and paint liveries. As a result most postwar diesel-electric fleets were composed of standardized, interchangeable models, instead of specialized machines. Railroads bought thousands of nearly identical Electro-Motive F-units, E-units, and GPs. Southern Pacific's "Tunnel Motor" was one of the few sig-

As the sun fades in the west, a Southern Pacific train led by an SD45T-2 and an SD40 roll across the high trestle at Redding, California. This profile view clearly shows the difference in length between the two locomotives. It also reveals the low-level air intakes on the SD45T-2 that make the locomotive significant. *Brian Solomon*

These Tunnel Motors are shoving hard in "run 8" (the highest throttle notch) working as the midtrain helper on Southern Pacific's MERVM (Medford, Oregon, to Roseville, California, manifest freight). The place is Talent, Oregon, just a few miles from Ashford; the time is April 1990. *Brian Solomon*

On February 4, 1994, Southern Pacific freights pass on the grade-separated mainline in the Truckee River Canyon near Floriston, California. This is the east slope of the famous Donner Pass grade. Interstate 80 is visible in the foreground. *Brian Solomon*

On January 16, 1993, a Rio Grande SD40T-2 leads the SNTAC unit coal train up Donner Pass at Floriston, California. *Brian Solomon*

yards and new freight lines, and gained international renown for hauling some of the fastest freights in the world. Like its neighbor, Union Pacific (which also inspired some distinctive locomotive designs, such as EMD's enormous dual-engine DDA40X), SP had encouraged locomotive builders to push the power limit. More power allowed the railroad to haul longer trains, and use fewer locomotives per train. In the early 1960s, SP purchased the largest fleet of diesel-hydraulics from German manufacturer Krauss-Maffei. The diesel-hydraulic locomotive promised greater horsepower and more tractive effort than domestic diesel-electrics. Initially SP seemed pleased at their potential, but it grew dissatisfied with the hydraulics' greater maintenance requirements and other problems.

In the mid-1960s, EMD introduced its most powerful single-engine diesel-electrics to date: the six-axle, six-motor, 3,000-horse-power SD40, and similar, but slightly more powerful 3,600-horse-power SD45. EMD's competition, General Electric and Alco, also offered similar high-horsepower, six-motor models. Southern Pacific was particularly impressed with these new machines and placed large orders for the SD40, and even larger orders for the SD45. It had by far the largest fleet of SD45s—357, including those for its Cotton

nificant exceptions in modern American diesel production. To meet its special requirements, SP got a fleet of distinctive locomotives, unlike those used on most other American lines.

By the 1960s, SP was one of America's most progressive freight railroads. It had transformed its system into an impressive freight hauler. While other American lines were downsizing, SP built new

Belt subsidiary. In general, SP was pleased with the performance of its SD45s, which remained with the railroad for three decades.

When EMD tested its 4,200-horsepower SD45X demonstrators on SP, it found inadequate performance when climbing in snowshed and tunnel territory on Donner Pass and in the Oregon Cascades. The problem was attributed to an airflow deficiency. On most EMDs, including the SD45, air intake vents are located at the top rear of the locomotive. Normally this doesn't cause any undue problems. When these big engines worked at full throttle in the confines of tunnels and snowsheds at high altitudes, however, they had a tendency to exhaust the available air supply, which caused the engines to overheat, degrading performance. To overcome this problem, Southern Pacific and EMD engineers worked together to redesign the locomotive airflow pattern. Air intake vents were relocated from the top of the locomotive to the level of the running boards. Satisfied with this, Southern Pacific ordered a fleet of specially designed six-motor EMDs in both 20-cylinder and 16-cylinder models, which, like the cab-ahead Mallets, were specially designed for operation in California's Sierras. These locomotives feature a "T" (for "tunnel") in their model designation. The 3,600-horsepower SD45T-2 was a variation of the SD45 and featured the 20-cylinder 645 engine, while the SD40T-2 was a variation of the SD40, using the 16-cylinder 645 engine. The first SD45T-2s were delivered in 1973, and the first SD40T-2s in 1974. The SD45T-2 was unique to SP; the SD40T-2 was also ordered by the Denver & Rio Grande Western, which had similar operating territory.

SP's Tunnel Motors were assigned heavy road duties all over its system, but were typically concentrated on its mountain lines out of

Roseville. They were often operated in tandem with SP's other big six-motor EMDs. Southern Pacific's Tunnel Motors were painted in its classic scarlet and gray livery, a paint scheme that looked sharp when clean, but was typically covered in layers of grime and grease. This reflected their harsh operating conditions and SP's lack of interest in washing locomotives, a situation that became particularly acute as the railroad's fortunes waned in the 1980s and 1990s.

In 1988, SP and Rio Grande came under common management, putting the two fleets of tunnel motors under common control. For the most part, Rio Grande's Tunnel Motors stayed in their home territory, although SP's roamed far and wide, on Rio Grande lines and elsewhere. In 1996, SP and Rio Grande merged with Union Pacific. While some Tunnel Motors had been sold for rebuilding, others joined the Union Pacific fleet, and a few were painted in UP's Armour yellow.

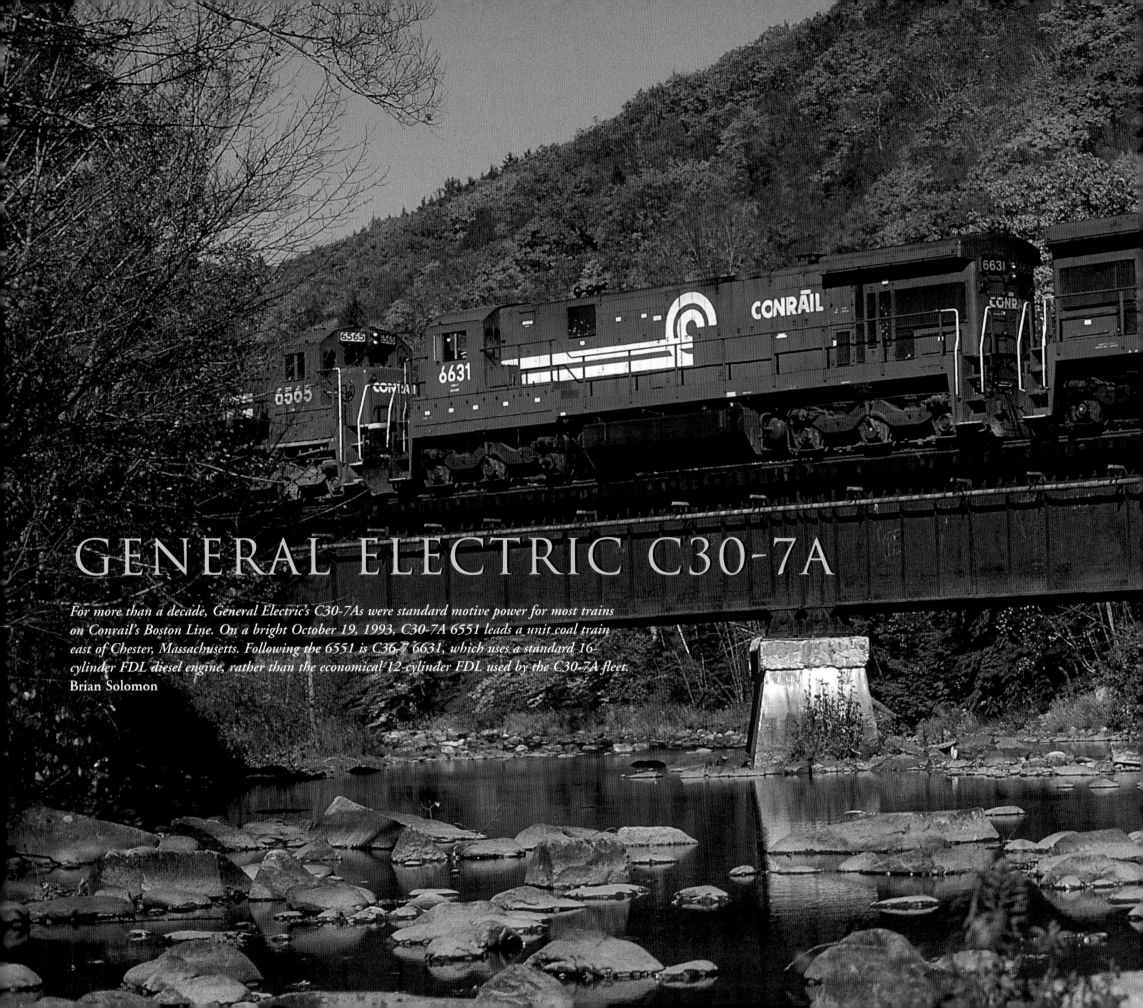

GENERAL ELECTRIC C30-7A

For more than a decade, General Electric's C30-7As were standard motive power for most trains on Conrail's Boston Line. On a bright October 19, 1993, C30-7A 6551 leads a unit coal train east of Chester, Massachusetts. Following the 6551 is C36-7 6631, which uses a standard 16-cylinder FDL diesel engine, rather than the economical 12-cylinder FDL used by the C30-7A fleet.
Brian Solomon

Conrail introduced the C30-7A to the Boston Line in 1984, assigning most of the 50-unit fleet to freight service between Boston and Selkirk, New York. At times the C30-7As roamed far and wide on Conrail, but they remained most common on the old B&A route. In September 1989, Conrail 6579 leads eastbound intermodal train TV6 through Palmer, Massachusetts.
Brian Solomon

GENERAL ELECTRIC C30-7A

General Electric's C30-7A was a relatively obscure model that shared some qualities with more common locomotives. While the C30-7A was only ordered by one railroad and just 50 of the type were built, it shared a family resemblance with other General Electric products. What made the C30-7A different was its unusual equipment configuration and other internal peculiarities. Despite its poor sales record, the locomotive proved to be a worthy machine with an excellent service record and an average life span.

General Electric introduced its first six-motor heavy-haul diesel in 1963 with its 2,500-horsepower U25C, essentially a six-axle version of its popular U25B (see page 84). Four years later, GE began production of the 3,000-horsepower U30C to compete with Electro-Motive's new SD40, which offered the same horsepower. During the 10 years the U30C remained in production, GE built 600 of them for North American service (592 were sold to American railroads, the remaining 8 to Mexico), making it by far the most numerous of the six-motor Universal (or "U-boat") line. As with GE's other high-horsepower heavy-haul locomotives, the U30C used General Electric's 16-cylinder FDL diesel engine.

In mid-1976, General Electric's DASH 7 line superseded the Universal line, and the C30-7 replaced the U30C in the 3,000-horsepower six-motor category. The DASH 7 line introduced a number of improvements to General Electric locomotives in an effort to compete more effectively with General Motor's Electro-Motive Division. While DASH 7 locomotives suffered from some quality control issues, the C30-7 was one of GE's best-selling locomotives. During the full decade it was in production, 1,137 of them were built for North American service, nearly twice as many as the U30C. The C30-7 closely resembled its 3,000-horsepower predecessor, but was distinguished by larger radiators at the back, known colloquially as "bat wings."

During the 1960s, General Electric developed a line of medium horsepower road switchers designated U23B and U23C, which used a 12-cylinder version of the FDL engine. The oil crisis in the 1970s sparked renewed interest in more fuel-efficient locomotives and made the FDL an attractive powerplant—the FDL's four-cycle design was inherently more fuel efficient than Electro-Motive's two-cycle engine. In 1980, Missouri Pacific asked GE to boost the output of its 12-cylinder FDL, resulting in the 3,000-horsepower B30-7A—the "A" distinguished this model as using a smaller engine than the standard 16-cylinder FDL. Cutting four cylinders significantly reduced fuel consumption on the high-horsepower road units, and General Electric fared very well with this concept. It sold 200 B30-7As, including 120 cabless "boosters" to Burlington Northern, during the model's three-year production run. This total is impressive, considering the United States was suffering a recession at the time, and thousands of older locomotives were stored all around the United States.

Conrail was especially hard hit by the recession, which caused its traffic to drop dramatically. Lines of stored locomotives at Conrail's massive Selkirk Yard near Albany, New York, stretched for miles. Hundreds of locomotives inherited from Conrail's bankrupt predecessor lines languished with their engine service doors banded shut, waiting for a traffic resurgence to bring them back to life. Among them were numerous older General Electric products, including U25Bs, U30Cs, U33Cs, and U36Cs. While the U25s had essentially run out of time, many of these other types were not that old, yet few of them would ever run again. Before the recession hit, Conrail had ordered hundreds of new road locomotives from Electro-Motive and General Electric in the late 1970s, and it was this newer, more reliable power that Conrail relied upon for the bulk of its through service. Among the locomotives Conrail acquired from GE were a sizable fleet of B23-7s, which employed the 12-cylinder FDL to generate 2,300 horsepower, and 10 16-cylinder C30-7s.

In 1983, the economy started to rebound, and Conrail's traffic picked up, encouraging it to order new locomotives. While a few

LOCOMOTIVE FACTS

MODEL:	GENERAL ELECTRIC C30-7A
WHEEL ARRANGEMENT:	C-C
ENGINE TYPE:	7FDL-12
HORSEPOWER:	3,000
YEAR BUILT:	1984
NUMBER BUILT:	50
TRANSMISSION:	DC

stored locomotives were plucked from the dead lines, these were primarily Electro-Motive products. New locomotives featured more reliable and more fuel-efficient designs. In late 1983 and early 1984, Conrail received 130 SD50s from Electro-Motive and 60 B36-7s from General Electric, both of which were standard models.

Then in mid-1984, General Electric built the fleet of hybrid C30-7As for Conrail, a model that combined the successful six-motor C30-7 locomotive with the high-horsepower, fuel-efficient 12-cylinder FDL engine. The C30-7A model was intended for a high tractive effort, moderate-speed application with good fuel efficiency as a significant objective. They were assigned to Selkirk Yard for service on the rugged Boston Line, the former Boston & Albany mainline, a route well known for its tough operating conditions.

A quartet of 12-cylinder FDLs make music as they lift a heavy westbound over Washington Hill near Middlefield, Massachusetts, on July 19, 1997. Each of these locomotives generates 96,900 pounds continuous tractive effort operating at 8.8 miles per hour, and this day they needed every pound of that power to get over the Boston Line's most formidable grade. *Brian Solomon*

Trains have to surmount three summits on this 200-mile route. The most difficult of these is Washington Hill, located in the Berkshire Hills of western Massachusetts between Pittsfield and Springfield. Here the westbound ruling grade is 1.67 percent (a climb of 1.67 feet for every 100 feet traveled). This is not nearly as steep as other mainlines, particularly those in the West, where long 2.2 percent grades are common and grades as steep as 3 percent are not unheard off. The Boston Line is made especially difficult by the combination of steep gradients and numerous sharp curves that follow a sinuous profile up and down the mountains.

Freights roll along at respectable speed on the more level tangent segments of the Boston Line, but they grind to a crawl when they reach Washington Hill—the most difficult section of the whole railroad, a few miles between Chester, Massachusetts, and the summit at Washington.

This grade has been a proving ground for locomotive designs since the 1840s, and it defines train makeup and motive power needs for the whole route. On a dry day, a freight might slug it out at 5 or 10 miles per hour, as it crawls up through the deep rock cuts above Chester. But on a wet day, or worse a snowy day, locomotives

Conrail C30-7A pauses at Chester, Massachusetts, on August 13, 1988. *Brian Solomon*

can easily loose traction, slip, and stall. Many a knuckle has been broken, and many drawbars pulled at milepost 129 (marking the distance from Boston), where the grade is at its toughest. Traditionally heavy freights attacking Washington Hill were assigned helpers at Chester. These helpers would shove trains over the mountain to Washington Summit at Hinsdale or beyond to Pittsfield, minimizing the chance of stalling. In 1982, Conrail issued an edict mandating that trains on the Boston Line were to be sufficiently powered, and eliminated the Washington Hill helpers. This was part of a trend toward more streamlined operations on Conrail. In early 1984, prior to the delivery of the C30-7As, Conrail began running cabooseless through freights on the Boston Line, ending another traditional railroad practice. Conrail management took these actions to reduce operating costs and make the railroad profitable, a goal it ultimately achieved.

The 50 C-307As were followed shortly by 10 C32-8s, pre-production units that were a precursor to GE's successful DASH 8 line introduced a few years later. Like the C30-7As, the C32-8s employed the 12-cylinder FDL engine, making the two locomotive models near cousins, despite using different body styles. Conrail initially made an effort to operate solid sets of three C30-7As or C32-8s, yet it didn't take long before the two models were mixed together on Boston Line freights. These two high-horsepower models were the only GE six-axles sold in the United States with 12-cylinder prime movers, although GE marketed the 12-cylinder, six-axle concept for export. The DASH 7 line remained part of GE's export catalog many years after the construction of the Conrail locomotives and introduction of successively more power locomotives.

The C30-7As were standard Boston Line power for 15 years. The early sets of three eventually gave way to standard sets of four locomotives. This provided 12,000 horsepower for lifting freight over the Berkshires, which seemed to be enough to move the lengths and weight of trains that Conrail wanted to operate. At times it seemed that the C30-7As were assigned to Boston Line freights to the exclusion of all other power, as the very same locomotives would roll day in and day out between Selkirk and Boston. In fact, the C30-7As could be found all over Conrail. In the 1990s, Conrail retired its fleet of aging U23Cs, which had worked humps at Enola, Pennsylvania, Selkirk, and other places, and assigned GE C30-7As for this work.

In 1999, CSX and Norfolk Southern split up Conrail and divided its assets. The C30-7A fleet was split between the two railroads. Shortly after it assumed operations, CSX assigned its fleet of AC6000CWs to Boston line, displacing the C30-7As and other power. As fairly unusual locomotives, the C30-7As didn't appear to have a long future with their new owners. Less than two years after the Conrail breakup, all of the C30-7As had been withdrawn from service and placed in storage at Enola Yard to await disposition.

GENERAL ELECTRIC DASH 9

Chicago & North Western purchased the first DASH 9s in December 1993. Three clean C&NW DASH 9-44CWs lead a Powder River coal train eastward through Creston, Illinois, on April 2, 1995.
Brian Solomon

Burlington Northern Santa Fe DASH 9 No. 1116 leads an eastbound freight at Sais, New Mexico. General Electric's DASH 9 line reflects a host of improvements on its already successful DASH 8 locomotive design. The DASH 9 has remained a popular locomotive type on North American railways despite the advances in alternating current traction motor technology. *Brian Solomon*

GENERAL ELECTRIC DASH 9

Through the 1960s and 1970s, General Electric played second fiddle to General Motor's Electro-Motive Division in the locomotive business. The industry seemed to feel that EMD's locomotives were more reliable than GE's, and EMD outsold GE in all major categories. In the late 1970s, GE introduced its DASH 7 line, reflecting a number of design improvements over its Universal line, which had debuted with the U25B (see General Electric U25B, page 84). GE sold a large number of DASH 7s (see General Electric C30-7A, page 108), but its sales still lagged behind EMD's.

During the early 1980s, General Electric made a serious effort to improve its product line and designed a significantly better locomotive. In 1982, it began developing microprocessor-controlled locomotives that would change the whole industry. The advent of microprocessor control is now considered the beginning of the "third generation"—the first generation being those machines that displaced steam, and the second being the wave of high-horsepowered locomotives that replaced the first-generation diesels. (These categories were created after the fact by locomotive chronologists and historians; the actual transition from one generation to the next is characterized by a logical sequence of incremental improvements, and there are numerous examples of overlapping technology.)

General Electric's microprocessor prototypes led to GE's DASH 8 locomotive line. The "DASH 7" designation reflected 1970s technology, and consequently, DASH 8 had a connotation of 1980s technology. The first DASH 8 locomotives were pre-production units that were built between 1984 and 1987, alongside standard DASH 7s. Today, these early DASH 8s are known as "Classics." They are characterized by a distinctive contoured cab profile that gives the locomotive something of a humpback appearance, hence their nickname, "camels."

The DASH 8 is interesting to look at, but its microprocessor control is what sets it apart from its contemporaries. The onboard microprocessor in the DASH 8 optimizes performance by obtaining information from a variety of sources and providing calculated control of engine speed, cooling functions, and wheel slip in response, thus offering a degree of precision not available through traditional means. The microprocessor collects and compares data such as the manifold air pressure, engine speed, traction motor current, axle speed, and train speed, as well as the positions of the engineer's controls, and uses preprogrammed software strategies to automatically regulate locomotive outputs. In addition, the microprocessor provides a digital recording system of locomotive functions and provides detailed diagnostic tools in case of a failure or poor locomotive performance.

The purpose of the new technology was to produce a more efficient machine, with greater power potential, higher reliability, and lower emissions than earlier designs. Conrail, Santa Fe, Burlington Northern, and Norfolk Southern operated Classic DASH 8s in daily service, which provided field experience to help GE refine the design of its microprocessor control before introducing production locomotives. Finally, after three years of field testing, GE debuted its "Enhanced" DASH 8 line for regular production

General Electric's Enhanced DASH 8 was a vastly improved machine that soon became its best-selling locomotive, allowing GE to surpass EMD as the world's foremost diesel-electric supplier and retain the top position for years. While the Enhanced DASH 8's fundamental components—GE's 7-FDL four-cycle diesel engine, GE752 direct current traction motors, and GMG alternator—remained unchanged, the new model featured a number of internal and external differences that distinguished it from earlier models. On the outside, the contour cab used on the early Classics had given way to a boxy, utilitarian design. Inside, an improved electrical system and other refinements gave the model significantly better reliability than older GE locomotives.

General Electric built several DASH 8 models for North American service. It built DASH 8 in four- and six-axle models, with both medium- and high-horsepower output for both freight and passenger road designs. While the DASH 8 line was in production, GE introduced a number of incremental improvements and options to the line. For example, in the late 1980s when American railroads expressed an interest in wide-nose safety cabs, GE offered the wide cab as an option. By 1993, GE had introduced enough design options and improvements to justify a new name, the DASH 9.

The DASH 9 was initially built as one basic model, the DASH 9-44CW. This six-axle 4,400-horsepower locomotive uses six direct current traction motors, features the standard General Electric wide-nose safety cab, and incorporates several new standard features, some

In September 1998, a westbound BNSF train at Abo Canyon, New Mexico, features three DASH 9-44CW locomotives, each wearing a different color scheme—a legacy of the merger of the Burlington Northern and the Santa Fe in 1995. *Brian Solomon*

Norfolk Southern has ordered hundreds of DASH 9-44CWs for both heavy coal and intermodal service around its system. A pair of NS DASH 9s lead an eastbound intermodal train through Cresson, Pennsylvania, on September 30, 2000. *Brian Solomon*

of which were available as options on DASH 8 models. The DASH 9 uses high-adhesion trucks, split cooling, electronic fuel injection, and improved ergonomic steps. The high-adhesion truck was the only improvement not used on DASH 8 locomotives. It was a new bolsterless truck designed to reduce weight transfer and allow for easier maintenance. (A truck bolster is a mechanical weight-bearing surface on which the wheels pivot beneath the locomotive body.) By reducing the weight transfer, this truck improves wheel-to-rail adhesion. The high-adhesion truck is identifiable by its boxy, uncluttered appearance and winged journal boxes. It has remained a standard feature on GE's 4,400-horsepower alternating traction locomotives that were introduced after the DASH 9. Despite its entirely different propulsion system, the AC4400CW looks very much the same as the DASH 9, leading to some confusion when identifying locomotives.

Split cooling is one of the DASH 9's selling features. This system uses radiators with two independent water circuits for the engine intercoolers. By improving intercooler performance, GE reduced air intake temperature, which lowered engine emissions. In addition to the split

cooling circuit, GE also introduced a new crankcase ventilation system that uses a coalescer to remove lube oil vapors from engine exhaust. The coalescer works as a filter through which vapors are passed to collect oil droplets. The split cooling system is identifiable by noticeably thicker radiator "wings" than used by earlier DASH 8 locomotives.

Electronic fuel injection (EFI) replaced the mechanical fuel injection used on earlier diesel engines. EFI optimizes engine combustion by electronically varying fuel injection timing, automatically. This results in better fuel economy, reduced exhaust emissions, improved reliability, and lower maintenance. EFI and split cooling were two important features for GE's customers, especially railroads operating in states with strict emission standards, such as California. Older locomotive designs were known for belching clouds of black smoke, causing some owners to be fined for pollution.

The spotting differences between late-model DASH 8 locomotives and the DASH 9 line are relatively minor, as many of the improvements incorporated in the DASH 9 can be found on late-built DASH 8s as well. There are even fewer external differences between the DASH 9 and the AC4400CW—GE's entry into the alternating current traction motor market. Further confusing matters, General Electric's model designations are not always used by the railroads, and many lines have invented their own model names. GE refers to its modern wide-cab, six-motor, DC traction locomotives as DASH 9-44CWs, but some customers use derivative designations based on earlier GE nomenclature, such as "C44-9W." Under either name, the locomotive is the same.

Despite the development of high-horsepower AC traction locomotives in the mid-1990s, the DASH 9 remained a popular model. Burlington Northern Santa Fe has ordered DASH 9s for general purpose use, often assigning them to intermodal runs and unit grain trains, while ordering new AC models for coal service. By contrast, Norfolk Southern has generally shunned new AC technology, preferring to use GE DASH 9-44CWs for both general manifest services and coal service.

ELECTRO-MOTIVE SD70MAC

Electro-Motive Division's SD70MAC was the first mass-produced diesel-electric locomotive to employ modern three-phase alternating current traction. Burlington Northern SD70MAC 9529 was brand new when this photo was made in 1995.
Brian Solomon

ELECTRO-MOTIVE SD70MAC

Electro-Motive's SD70MAC was a revolutionary locomotive for North American railroads. It was the first commercially produced diesel-electric locomotive built with three-phase alternating current (AC) traction motors, and it set the stage for a whole new generation of powerful new diesel electrics. Until the advent of the SD70MAC, all commercially mass-produced North American diesel-electric locomotives had employed conventional DC traction motors. The DC motor had been the most practical and efficient type of propulsion system since the diesel was introduced in the 1920s. Yet changes in the locomotive market and the emergence of new technology facilitated the development of practical three-phase AC traction.

Three-phase AC motors offer several distinct advantages that make them appealing for locomotive use. They are much simpler than comparable DC motors, require less maintenance, and can tolerate significantly rougher handling. Also they have greater output potential than DC motors of the same size. One of the most important characteristics of three-phase AC motors is their inherent ability to automatically correct for locomotive wheel slip, thereby significantly increasing adhesion. This gives a three-phase AC locomotive much greater tractive effort than a DC model, making AC especially desirable on steeply graded lines requiring greater pulling power. Despite three-phase AC's advantages, DC traction had long been preferred because of its ease of motor control. The development of adequate ways to control AC motors on a heavy-haul American locomotive changed the industry's perception of AC traction.

The history of AC traction goes back more than 100 years. The Gornergrat Railway in Switzerland was the first railway to employ a three-phase AC power system beginning about 1900. Shortly thereafter, several European electrical firms experimented with three-phase AC in high-speed applications. One of these test cars reached

LOCOMOTIVE FACTS

MODEL:	EMD SD70MAC
WHEEL ARRANGEMENT:	C-C
ENGINE TYPE:	16-710-G3B
HORSEPOWER:	4,000
YEARS BUILT:	1993 TO PRESENT
NUMBER BUILT:	IN PRODUCTION
TRANSMISSION:	AC

a top speed of 130.5 miles per hour (210 kilometers/hour). Unlike DC and single-phase AC, three-phase AC motors require three conductors, so the distribution of three-phase AC power for electric locomotives required a fairly complex arrangement, using multiple sets of overhead catenary wires and multiple pantographs. (Catenary is the network of overhead wires that deliver electric power for electric locomotives. A pantograph is the equipment on top of the locomotive that collects the current from the catenary.)

Despite the complexity of transmission, some heavily graded lines in Switzerland and Italy employed three-phase AC electrification. Eventually, Italy boasted more than 1,000 miles of three-phase AC lines, the most of any country in the world. Portions of Italy's three-phase AC electrification survived until the 1970s, when it was finally replaced by more practical transmission systems.

Three-phase overhead power was not exclusive to Europe. In the United States, the Great Northern's original Stevens Pass electrification over the Washington Cascades employed a three-phase system. While considered successful, this system was relatively short-lived. Advances in DC traction nullified the slight advantages of the AC systems, so when GN extended its electrification in the 1920s, it switched over to DC. This system remained in place until the

◀ *Previous Page*
Three SD70MACs lead a unit coal train near the summit of Nebraska's Crawford Hill at Belmont, Nebraska, on May 29, 1995. Burlington Northern applied its "Executive" scheme to its new SD70MACs to distinguish them from conventional DC traction locomotives. (The scheme's forest green color has a tendency to reproduce as black in photographs.) *Brian Solomon*

◀ Two sets of SD70MACs lead unit coal trains loading at Wyoming's enormous Black Thunder Mine. Today BNSF, and its competitor, Union Pacific, move more than 100 loaded coal trains a day out of the Powder River Basin, making it one of the best places to watch and photograph modern locomotives. *Brian Solomon*

▼ Three SD70MACs were designed to do the same work as five SD40-2s and thus offer a great cost savings to the railroad. On May 26, 1995, Burlington Northern SD70MACs lead an eastbound unit coal train at Burdock, South Dakota. *Brian Solomon*

► Crawford Hill in far northwestern Nebraska is a tough climb for eastbound Powder River coal trains. Here Burlington Northern must assign rear-end helpers to get trains over the hill. Even with three SD70MACs on the point and another two or three on the rear, a typical coal train would grind up the grade at just 5 to 10 miles per hour. *Brian Solomon*

▼ Two glistening new SD70MACs lead a loaded coal train into the yards at Cumberland, Maryland, on September 25, 1997. Pairs of the AC traction locomotives were used to haul loaded coal trains east of Grafton, West Virginia, over the old Baltimore & Ohio "West End," a heavily graded mainline now known as the Mountain Subdivision. *Brian Solomon*

service, with a maximum speed of 100 miles per hour. Using three-phase AC, this four-axle machine produced 76,440 pounds tractive effort, which was greater than comparable six-axle, six-motor DC electric locomotives. While the Class 120 never fully met expectations, it was a nominal success, and many were built for service in Germany, many of which are still in regular service (as of 2001).

Manufacturers further developed three-phase AC in the 1980s, aiming toward high-speed rail applications. By the early 1990s, AC traction was in use on high-speed trains in Germany, France, and Japan. AC traction was used to reduce the number of motors required to move a high-speed train, which could now reach top operating speeds of 186 miles per hour (300 kilometers/hour)—much faster than anything in the United States.

North American railroads had a different interest in modern three-phase AC technology, viewing it primarily as a way of moving heavy tonnage with greater efficiency. Successful three-phase AC motors in Europe and Japan led General Motor's Electro-Motive Division to experiment with applying the technology to a diesel-electric locomotive. In the early 1990s, EMD equipped a pair of four-axle locomotives, designated Model F69PHAC, with three-phase electrical equipment as a test. EMD next built a quartet of three-phase AC six-axle, six-motor demonstrators, based on the successful SD60M DC traction design. These were designated SD60MAC, dressed in a modified Burlington Northern paint scheme, and tested in heavy coal service.

By the early 1990s, BN had become one of the largest coal-hauling railroads in North America as a result of its mines in Wyoming's Powder River Basin. By this time it was hauling an estimated 150 million tons of coal a year. Most coal trains were hauled by quintets

1950s, when GN abandoned electrified operations altogether in favor of through diesel-electric operations.

During the 1970s, there was a renewed interest in three-phase AC traction in Germany. By this time, advances in thyristor and microprocessor technology had made simulated three-phase AC power possible. Simulated AC eliminated the need for complex overhead electrical transmission. Instead, power could be drawn from conventional single-phase AC overhead power, converted to DC power and then inverted using thyristors to create polyphase AC power. Motor control was accomplished by modulating AC frequency.

In 1979, following several years of testing, the first modern, commercially built, three-phase AC overhead-electric locomotive was delivered to Deutsche Bundesbahn (West German Federal Railways). It was designated the Class 120 and intended for dual

In 1995, Burlington Northern merged with the Santa Fe to form one of America's largest railroad systems. Following the merger, BNSF experimented with a variety of paint schemes before settling on the "Heritage II" scheme, seen here on SD70MAC No. 8955 at Walsenburg, Colorado, in June 2000. *Mike Gardner*

In the fading glow of sunset, Burlington Northern SD70MACs roll eastward with a long coal train in tow. *Brian Solomon*

of conventional 3,000-horsepower, six-motor DC traction diesels, usually EMD SD40-2s or General Electric C30-7s. The greater tractive effort afforded by AC traction presented BN with the possibility of replacing five 3,000-horsepower DC diesels with just three 4,000-horsepower, three-phase AC traction locomotives, representing a significant cost savings. Following successful tests with the SD60MACs, BN placed an order for hundreds of AC locomotives with EMD, giving the locomotive manufacturer the financial incentive to perfect the technology. Using its experience, EMD developed the SD70MAC, which incorporated several other modern innovations in addition to AC traction.

The first BN SD70MACs were delivered at the end of 1993, and hundreds more followed. Burlington Northern—and its successor company, Burlington Northern Santa Fe (the result of a merger with Santa Fe in 1995)—has enjoyed excellent service from its enormous fleet of SD70MACs. The success of this design sparked a revolution in motive power. Both Electro-Motive Division, and its competitor, General Electric, have introduced a variety of high tractive effort three-phase AC traction diesels. While DC traction is still preferred for some applications, thousands of AC traction locomotives are now in heavy service throughout North America.

The SD70MAC employs a 16-cylinder 710G prime mover that generates 4,000 horsepower, just 200 horsepower more than a DC traction SD60M. The advantages of the locomotive are not obtained from its powerful diesel engine, but from the modern three-phase AC traction system. The SD70MAC uses modern microprocessor and semiconductor technology developed by the German electrical firm, Siemens AG, which produced AC propulsion systems for high-speed trains in Europe. Banks of inverters use high-amperage gate turnoff thyristors (GTOs) to convert DC power to modulated three-phase AC power. (A GTO serves as an on/off switch that converts DC power into an emulated sine wave that is manipulated to control motor output.) The greater adhesion afforded by the SD70MAC's traction motors corrects for wheel slip, giving the locomotive significantly greater tractive power. A DC traction SD60M enjoys just 25 percent adhesion and develops an estimated 100,000 pounds of maximum continuous tractive effort. By comparison, the SD70MAC enjoys 33 percent adhesion and develops an estimated 137,000 pounds of maximum continuous tractive effort.

One of the SD70MAC's greatest selling points is its sustained ability to work under full load without risk of damage to its traction motors, a quality that separates it from all previous American diesel-electric designs. DC traction models risk damaging traction motors by overloading them for long periods of time.

One innovation used on the SD70MAC that is not directly related to its propulsion system is its HTCR "radial truck," a self-steering truck designed to reduce friction between driving wheels and the rails, minimizing wear to both surfaces.

The SD70MAC's ability to lug for extended periods is especially advantageous in hauling extremely heavy trains over steep mountain grades, and this is where most SD70MACs earn their keep.

EMD CLASS 66

On the afternoon of April 6, 2000, English Welsh & Scottish Railway 66029 leads a freight through Oxford. Although the railway operation is in Britain, the Class 66 is a very American locomotive. It was built in North America, using American technology, for an American-controlled railway, with an American paint scheme. Brian Solomon

EMD CLASS 66

American locomotive builders have long enjoyed a healthy export trade. In the steam era, Baldwin and Alco had a robust business selling their machines overseas, and in times of lean domestic sales, it was often the export business that kept the locomotive builders alive. This trend has continued into the diesel era, and today both General Motors' Electro-Motive Division and General Electric produce a large number of locomotives for export. American diesel-electric locomotives are state-of-the-art machines, and considered the best worldwide. Recently this profound technological supremacy has been demonstrated in the United Kingdom, where hundreds of new EMDs are now in service.

Britain invented both the railway and the steam engine, and for more than a century and a half, it exported locomotives around the world. In the early days of steam, American railways imported British-built locomotives. Britain waited until the 1950s to dieselize its operations, but once it made this decision, British locomotive manufacturers originated a variety of diesel designs. Some of the more impressive models have included English Electric's high-speed Deltic. This locomotive was designed for 100-mile per hour operation, using a pair of 18-cylinder, triangular configured, opposed piston, Napier-Deltic diesel engines. Another successful English Electric product is the Type 3, Class 37—a six-axle, general purpose locomotive with a 1,750-horsepower engine. Between 1960 and 1966, 240 of these machines were built, and some

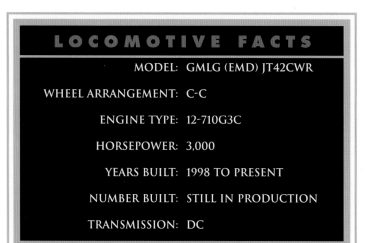

▲ A pair of Class 66s roll through Crewe on the West Coast Mainline. This heavily traveled electrified route connects London with Birmingham, Manchester, and Glasgow. It is not one line, but a group of lines. The English Welsh & Scottish Railway provides freight service over this line and most others in Britain. *Brian Solomon*

▸ On a typical dreary English afternoon, a English Welsh & Scottish Class 66 leads a westbound freight through the station at Bath Spa. This route was once on Isambard K. Brunel's famous "Broad Gauge," a line built with tracks 7 feet, 1/4 inch wide. Today this line uses the Stephenson Standard Gauge (4 feet, 8 1/2 inches). *Brian Solomon*

LOCOMOTIVE FACTS	
MODEL:	GMLG (EMD) JT42CWR
WHEEL ARRANGEMENT:	C-C
ENGINE TYPE:	12-710G3C
HORSEPOWER:	3,000
YEARS BUILT:	1998 TO PRESENT
NUMBER BUILT:	STILL IN PRODUCTION
TRANSMISSION:	DC

have survived in service through the year 2000. In the mid-1970s, British Rail introduced 125-mile per hour passenger service, using its HST (High Speed Train), a train powered by a pair of Class 43 streamlined diesel-electrics, one at each end of the train. Each Class 43 uses a 12-cylinder Paxman-Valenta engine, generating 2,250 horsepower. In tests the HST achieved 143 miles per hour, and regularly operates at its specified 125-mile per hour maximum speed, which gives it the title of the fastest diesel-electric in the world. Despite these notable successes, railway operators in Britain have largely turned their back on domestic diesel-electric designs in favor of American locomotive technology.

World War II bombing devastated railways in Britain, and in 1948 the four large private railways (grouped from dozens of smaller companies in 1923) were nationalized under the banner of British Rail. In the early 1990s, the British government moved to break up British Rail and privatize it. The system of privatization did not follow a conventional path. Rather than sell trains and tracks along different routes to different companies, BR separated the railway infrastructure from the railway services and sold the tracks to one company, and railway operating franchises to more than two dozen different companies.

In 1996, the majority of British freight operations came under the control of an American-led franchise, English, Welsh & Scottish Railway, a company led by Ed Burkhardt, the genius behind the success of Wisconsin Central. (The Wisconsin Central was a regional freight railroad formed in the mid-1980s from secondary routes spun off by the Soo Line, which had just merged with Milwaukee Road. Burkhardt transformed the Wisconsin Central routes into one of the greatest success stories of the American railroad industry.) One of Burkhardt's first actions on assuming charge of operations in Britain was to order 250 new locomotives for EWS, one of the largest single orders for new locomotives in Britain since the steam era. A longtime user of Electro-Motive products, Burkhardt placed his order with EMD. While this invasion of American diesels shocked some in the British railway industry, it was not unprecedented.

In 1985, the aggregate mover, Foster Yeoman, ordered a small fleet of EMDs to haul its stone trains. Designated Class 59, these were dual-cab, bidirectional diesels (the standard format for most road diesels in Britain) based on the successful EMD SD40-2. The Class 59 was powered by a 3,300-horsepower, 16-cylinder 645E3C engine. (In American terms, this translates to a 3,000-horsepower locomotive.) The success of the Class 59 led another aggregate company to make a similar purchase in the mid-1990s.

EMD's challenge in designing the Class 66, a locomotive that externally looks very similar to the Class 59, was adapting its successful SD70 design to accommodate Britain's restrictive loading gauge, weight, and noise requirements. Service requirements are very different in Britain than they are in the United States. In Britain, the railways generally feature more gentle grades and virtually no long extended climbs, as do railways in the United States. British freight trains are much shorter and lighter than their American counterparts, but are typically expected to operate on lines that also accommodate large numbers of tightly scheduled passenger trains. Delays to passenger trains because of slow-moving freights are much less acceptable in Britain than in America, so the freights must be able to easily negotiate passenger schedules. American railroads typically assign two or more locomotives to freights, but in Britain it is rare that more than two locomotives would be used to haul a single train, and it is quite common to assign a single locomotive to a scheduled mainline freight. Single-unit operation is one of the reasons for the dual-cab arrangement found on British locomotives.

In America, large numbers of level highway crossings have only the most rudimentary protection. In the interest of crew safety, American locomotives typically feature a substantial long nose in front of the cab, to protect crews in the event of a collision. Furthermore, the most modern locomotives are typically equipped with wide-nose "safety cabs," giving train crews added protection. A different philosophy prevails in Britain; the crew generally rides directly at the front of the locomotive. This is less of a safety concern, because the chance of a grade crossing accident is much less likely in Britain. There are far fewer level crossings, and crossings typically have much more elaborate protection systems than in America. Additionally, a history of fencing off railway right of ways discourages people and animals from trespassing on the tracks. Also, virtually all lines in Britain feature protective train control signaling. The front end cab arrangement facilitates coupling; it is a great advantage for the locomotive crew to be able to see the wagons (railway cars) as they connect to them.

Like the Class 59, the Class 66 generates 3,300 horsepower and delivers 3,000 horsepower to the rail. However, the Class 66 uses a state-of-the-art 12-cylinder 710 diesel engine, instead of the older 16-cylinder 645 used in the Class 59. The Class 66 also uses the modern HTCR self-steering radial truck, designed for use on the SD70MAC. This modern truck greatly reduces wheel and rail friction. Compared to EMD's domestic SD70, the Class 66 is a very compact machine. To accommodate weight restrictions, EMD needed to employ lighter weight alternators and traction motors, and use a much smaller fuel tank than on the SD70.

Between 1998 and 2000, EMD built 250 Class 66s at its London, Ontario, facility, shipping them by sea to Britain, where they were quickly dispatched into a variety of EWS freight services. Their exceptional reliability, and roughly 95 percent availability, is significantly better than comparable British-built diesels. Since EWS's original order, Britain's other large freight carrier, Freightliner, which primarily handles intermodal shipments, has ordered a small fleet of Class 66s, and recently there has been interest from other European railways as well.

GENERAL ELECTRIC AC6000CW

General Electric's AC6000CW is one of the most powerful diesel-electric locomotives in the world. A single AC6000CW has more horsepower than a four-unit EMD FT set built during World War II. In October 2000, a pair of CSX AC6000CWs lead a westbound freight over the Quaboag River at West Warren, Massachusetts. Brian Solomon

General Electric AC6000CW

The rural Quaboag River Valley east of Palmer, Massachusetts, reverberates with the sounds of power, a chortling, base chug that rolls up the valley ahead of an eastbound CSX intermodal train. Here the rails of the former Boston & Albany quiver beneath the wheels of the latest and greatest diesel locomotive offered by General Electric, today one of the world's premier locomotive manufacturers. When one thinks of the Boston & Albany, images of its great 2-8-4 Berkshires come to mind, those wondrous machines that Lima built in the mid-1920s that changed the way American railroads looked at steam. The Berkshire was so much more powerful than anything else on the line. With its huge firebox, the 2-8-4 could lift a heavy train over the Berkshire Hills—for which it was named—faster and more fuel efficiently than anything on the railroad. The Berkshire type displaced most of the older road power on the Boston & Albany. The 2-6-6-2 Mallets, 2-10-2 Santa Fes, and even relatively new 2-8-2 Mikados stepped aside for the powerful Berkshire. Today the image of those fine steam locomotives is preserved in photos and stories, and a new breed of power takes the tonnage over the hills and through the valleys served by the old B&A route.

For the moment, the AC6000CW is the power of choice on the Boston Line—as the B&A is now known—and these locomotives, like the old Berkshires, are more powerful and more fuel efficient than just about anything else around. On the Boston Line, two new 6,000-horsepower General Electric units effectively replace four of the older 3,000-horsepower General Electric C30-7As that had spent the previous 15 years moving freight over the B&A route (see page 108).

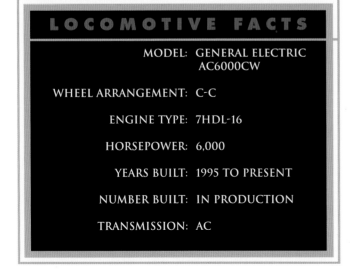

LOCOMOTIVE FACTS	
MODEL:	GENERAL ELECTRIC AC6000CW
WHEEL ARRANGEMENT:	C-C
ENGINE TYPE:	7HDL-16
HORSEPOWER:	6,000
YEARS BUILT:	1995 TO PRESENT
NUMBER BUILT:	IN PRODUCTION
TRANSMISSION:	AC

In 1993, the Electro-Motive Division ushered in the AC traction era with its SD70MAC (see page 118), but General Electric was not far behind with its own AC traction locomotive. To support its research efforts, GE, like EMD, needed a railroad to place a significant order for AC traction locomotives. With EMD, this had been the coal-hauling Burlington Northern, and with General Electric it was coal-hauling CSX. In 1993, CSX gave GE the largest single order for new locomotives it ever had. Some of these were traditional DC traction locomotives, but the majority were new AC traction power. The first General Electric AC was its AC4400CW, which matched the horsepower output of its existing DASH 9 design (see page 114),but offered significantly higher tractive effort. Later ACs still within the original CSX order were an all-new high-horsepower design that delivered a whopping 6,000 horsepower per locomotive, significantly more than offered by any conventional DC design.

General Electric was very successful with its AC4400CW, a model that made its debut in 1994. Hundreds were sold to a variety of American railroads for heavy service, and they quickly became a preferred model for hauling coal trains. Southern Pacific, Union Pacific, Chicago & North Western, Canadian Pacific, and CSX placed orders for the AC4400CW. One of the principal differences between General Electric's AC locomotives and EMD's is the arrangement of the inverters to the traction motors. An inverter is the electrical equipment that produces simulated three-phase AC current to power the traction motors, an integral part of the AC traction system. On an EMD, such as the SD70MAC, there are just two inverters, one for each truck. On a GE, there are six inverters, one for each traction motor. This difference is significant, because with the GE system a single inverter failure results in the locomotive losing power to a single traction motor, while on an EMD an inverter failure results in a loss of power to three of the six motors, or 50 percent of the locomotive's total output.

Several advantages of AC traction made it appealing to CSX and other lines. The combination of new microprocessor technology and AC traction motors resulted in a much higher level of adhesion than was possible with older DC traction locomotives. AC traction

motors afford better wheel slip control, which means the locomotive can apply more power to the rail for higher efficiency and more pulling power. A traditional DC locomotive would have just 18 to 25 percent adhesion, while, according to General Electric, a new AC6000CW obtains 39.5 percent adhesion. The AC6000CW delivers a maximum 180,000 pounds of starting tractive effort, and 166,000 pounds of continuous tractive effort at 11.6 miles per hour.

General Electric's AC4400CW shares many principal components with its DC cousin, the DASH 9. These locomotives use the same prime mover, the 7FDL16, which uses a design that dates back to GE's pioneering U25B (see page 84). They sit on the same frame, and feature the same wide-nose safety cab. To the untrained observer, there appears to be very little difference between the DASH 9 and the AC4400CW, despite the fact that they have entirely different traction systems and offer very different performance. This is not the case with the AC6000CW. It is a very different machine. It uses a new larger carbody—76 feet long, or 2 feet, 10 inches longer than the AC4400CW—with much larger radiators than any earlier GE design. The massive wings at the rear of the locomotive house the radiators, which are designed to accommodate 550 gallons of coolant.

The reason for the larger carbody, and the need for the larger radiators, is very simple. The AC6000CW, unlike virtually all other GE road locomotives since the U25B, does not use the Cooper-Bessemer-designed 7FDL engine. To obtain the 6,000 horsepower necessary to power this locomotive, GE needed a new engine design, so it teamed up with the German engine manufacturer, Deutz MWM, and built a new diesel engine, called the GE 7HDL. Like earlier GE engines, the 7HDL is a four-cycle design. It is in a 45-degree "V" configuration, operates at 1,050 rpm, and features a 15:1 compression ratio. Unlike 7FDL, which had gradually evolved and was adapted to drive increasingly more powerful locomotives, the 7HDL was designed for the AC6000.

Union Pacific was the other railroad initially interested in the AC6000CW. Perpetually power hungry, but unwilling to wait until the new 7HDL engine had been developed, Union Pacific ordered a number of "convertible" locomotives from GE. These locomotives featured the larger carbody, but were initially powered with the older 4,400-horsepower 7FDL engine. As soon as the new engine was perfected, they could easily be upgraded to that powerplant. This was another case of things not being what they appear—an all-too-common scenario in the world of modern locomotives.

General Electric delivered its first AC6000CW prototypes to CSX in 1998. CSX put the new locomotives through rigorous testing in coal and freight service on its heavily graded Mountain subdivision between Cumberland, Maryland, and Grafton, West Virginia. This territory, long the bastion of big EMD power, gave CSX and GE the

On March 10, 1996, a trio of new Union Pacific "convertibles" lead a Powder River coal train at Henry, Nebraska. In the mid-1990s, Union Pacific desperately needed new motive power, so it took delivery of locomotives with the old 7FDL engine, but ones that were designed to accommodate the new 6,000-horsepower engine when it became available. *Tom S. Hoover*

In the fading light of a fall afternoon, a pair of AC6000CWs roll eastward through West Brimfield, Massachusetts. Two AC6000CWs can do the same work as four EMD SD40-2s or GE C307As. *Brian Solomon*

opportunity to work out problems as they developed, while keeping the locomotives in captive service. Unlike the AC4400CW, the AC6000CW was better suited to intermodal and manifest service than heavy drag work. So when production AC6000CWs were finally ready for road work, many of them were not assigned to coal duties, but went to work in the regular road pool.

Another development that transpired while the AC6000CW was being perfected was the splitting up of Conrail between eastern rivals, CSX and Norfolk Southern. Conrail was formed in 1976 from the bankrupt remnants of several large eastern railroads, including the vast Penn Central system. After more than 20 years, Conrail had been turned around and made not only a profitable railroad, but a highly desirable merger partner. In 1996 and 1997, CSX and NS had agreed to split up the Conrail network, with CSX largely getting former New York Central routes in the Northeast. The breakup went into effect in June 1999, and not long after that, CSX began deploying its new AC6000CW fleet on former Conrail lines. Today they are commonly found on a variety of CSX routes, typically operating in pairs in intermodal service. Likewise, Union Pacific AC6000CWs are operating on its routes, including those that it acquired through mergers with the Chicago & North Western and Southern Pacific.

ELECTRIC LOCOMOTIVES

The history of electric traction in America is a story of an unfulfilled dream. Although electrification has often been promoted as a more efficient method of moving trains, the cost of electrifying a railway line proved prohibitively high. A few routes in North America were electrified, but the diesel ultimately doomed most mainline electrification schemes, except for a few high density passenger operations and isolated mining railways. Despite the lack of electrified lines in America, the technology developed here has been exported around the world. Many of the basic principles established by American electric pioneers have been used as the basis for further development. An example is the Japanese Shinkansen, better known as the "Bullet Train." When this high-speed service was inaugurated in 1964 it amazed the world. The Japanese were operating the fastest trains in the world, traveling at a top speed of 135 miles per hour (they move much faster today). Yet they did this using the technology developed by American lines in the 1920s and 1930s.

Electric railway technology has come a long way in 100 years. Today many railways in Europe and Asia are electrified, and in some countries, such as Switzerland, electrified lines are predominant. Electric locomotive designs are the most advanced in the world. They are the fastest, most powerful, and by far the most efficient. Since North American railways and railway suppliers no longer have the edge in electric railway technology, when railroads have purchased electric locomotives in last few decades, they have turned to imported designs. The AEM-7 is derived from a Swedish prototype, while Amtrak's high-speed *Acela Express* uses a propulsion system designed for the French high-speed TGV system.

America now enjoys true high-speed electrification in the Northeast, where passenger trains routinely reach 150-miles per hour top speeds. Yet the vast majority of the American network still relies on diesel power. Some passenger trains are electrified, but

Old electrics never die, they just rust away. A few of New York Central's old S-motors survived as switchers in Grand Central until the early 1980s, making them the oldest continually serving locomotives in North America. Still lettered for Penn Central, No. 4715 had only been out of service for a few years when this photograph was made in 1989. *Brian Solomon*

On July 25, 1964, westbound Chicago-to-Seattle time freight No. 263 departs Three Forks, Montana, behind a pair of "Little Joes" and a GP9. In the 1950s, Milwaukee Road's electrical engineer, Lawrence Wylie, worked out a multiple-unit control that permitted the electrics and diesels to work together. The extra power afforded by the diesel allowed the Milwaukee to handle greater tonnage. *William D. Middleton*

virtually no one in the United States uses electric locomotives for long-distance freight. At one time a number of American railroads moved freight with electric locomotives, including the Pennsylvania Railroad, New Haven, New York Central, Boston & Maine, Virginian, Norfolk & Western, Great Northern, and the Milwaukee Road. But the transportation cost advantages of electrically operated freight were outweighed by the high cost of maintaining electrification and of allocating specialized fleets of locomotives that were expensive to build and could only operate in limited territory. The greater flexibility of diesel-electric locomotives, and the vast distances traversed by American lines account in large part for their dominance in the freight railroad network.

This section profiles five different electric locomotives. These give a broad chronological perspective, if not a good geographic one. Interestingly one of America's first electric locomotives has survived. Old New York Central No. 6000, later No. 100, which worked for more than six decades on New York Central's third rail electrification, was never scrapped. Sadly, it has not received the recognition that it deserves. Instead of occupying a premier spot in the Smithsonian Institution, it sits forlorn in a weed-grown yard south of Albany, New York, with other historic equipment. It is a tragedy that such a significant machine that has survived so long hasn't received better treatment. Some electrics have been preserved and properly displayed. Several of the Pennsylvania's GG1s are in museums, as well as other significant electrics, such as Milwaukee Road's pioneer boxcab electric, which is displayed in Duluth, Minnesota.

Electrics use the same basic system for designating wheel arrangement as diesels. However, many electrics used a combination of powered and unpowered axles in an articulated arrangement, where modern diesels tend to use primarily powered axles. Powered axles are counted in groups, represented by a letter, A for one axle, B for two, C for three, etc. Unpowered axles are counted with numbers in a straightforward fashion. Thus a GG1 electric with two unpowered axles, followed by two sets of three powered axles and another set of two unpowered axles, uses a 2-C+C-2 wheel arrangement. One other difference with electrics is their symmetrical arrangement. Most American diesels have a single cab, and are designed to operate directionally in multiple with other diesels. Electrics are almost always bidirectional with a cab at each end, and often operate singly.

◀ Amtrak AEM-7 915 accelerates out of the setting sun at Newark, Delaware, with one MHC (material handling car) and five Amfleet cars. Today the Northeast Corridor carries very little freight traffic, leaving the tracks free for fast, frequent passenger service. Most freight is accommodated on parallel lines. *Brian Solomon*

▲ On January 25, 2001, the Boston-bound *Acela Express* glides into New Haven, Connecticut, five minutes ahead of its scheduled departure time. Initially Amtrak offered just one *Acela Express* roundtrip. Additional services were to be added as more new trains came online. *Brian Solomon*

NEW YORK CENTRAL S-MOTOR

In their early years, the S-motors were used to haul all of New York Central's long-distance trains in and out of Grand Central. As Central acquired bigger and more powerful locomotives, the S-motor fleet was largely relegated to switching tasks. In the early 1960s, S2 No. 112 is seen at Mott Haven in The Bronx. Richard Jay Solomon

On a hazy summer afternoon, a pair of venerable S-motors switch at Mott Haven in The Bronx. To keep Grand Central Terminal free for suburban trains, most of New York Central's long-distance trains were assembled at Mott Haven. Today all of Amtrak's long-distance trains to New York City use Penn Station, leaving Grand Central strictly for Metro-North suburban trains. *Richard Jay Solomon*

LOCOMOTIVE FACTS	
RAILROAD:	NEW YORK CENTRAL
BUILDER:	GENERAL ELECTRIC/ALCO
MODEL/TYPE:	S2
WHEEL ARRANGEMENT:	2-D-2
HORSEPOWER:	NA
TRACTIVE EFFORT:	37,000
YEARS BUILT:	1906

NEW YORK CENTRAL S-MOTOR

By the turn of the twentieth century, New York City had become the nation's largest city, and it continued growing in leaps and bounds. Because of the city's rapid growth, New York Central's mainline to Manhattan Island suffered from burgeoning traffic levels. Not only did this primary passenger artery accommodate the Central's numerous long-distance and suburban trains, it also handled an ever-growing number of New Haven trains. The Central had enlarged its famous Grand Central Depot in 1898, yet by 1902 this great terminal was serving some 500 trains daily, and there was no end to the growth in sight.

Pollution from all steam locomotives was terrible. Making matters especially bad was the 2-mile Park Avenue Tunnel on the approach to Grand Central. This tunnel was often filled with dense smoke, making it hard to breathe and difficult for locomotive engineers to see. New York Central was pondering a radical solution to this problem—electrification—when catastrophe struck. On the morning of January 8, 1902, a loaded train, stopped at signal in the smoke-filled tunnel, was struck from behind by another inbound train that had overrun a smoke-obstructed stop signal. Wooden passenger cars splintered and burned in the collision, and 15 people were killed. The wreck precipitated a scandal, the public was furious, and laws were quickly passed forcing New York Central to electrify its entire New York terminal operations. This was a more difficult prospect than it may seem today. New York City was asking Central to do something that had never been done before: electrify a heavy mainline railroad. This was an awfully tall order and there was very little in the way of established technology. So New York Central suddenly found itself a pioneer in the new field of railway electrification. Although electricity had been employed extensively on city streetcar systems and intercity lines in the 1890s, the only example of mainline electrification in the United States was the B&O's short Baltimore Tunnel project of 1896.

New York Central assembled a team of the most talented engineers to develop a railway electrification plan. They included New York Central vice president William Wilgus, and electrification pioneer Frank Sprague, who had been the first to successfully develop an electric streetcar system. In less than four years, these talented men had pioneered a practical mainline electrification system. The project was done in conjunction with the design and building of a new, much larger Grand Central—the double-decked structure we know today as New York City's most famous terminal. Work began in 1903 and electrification was ready for revenue service in 1906.

A terrible accident in the Park Avenue Tunnels in 1902 pushed forward New York Central's decision to electrify its lines. This photo, made about 1907, shows an S-motor (then classified as a T-motor) at the old Grand Central Station. Notice the wooden passenger cars and the old shed behind the train. *Richard Jay Solomon collection*

weighed 200,500 pounds, and had a 35,500-pound axle loading. It was just 37 feet long, but could produce 32,000 pounds tractive effort. It delivered a continuous 2,200 horsepower, and in regular service the Class T could haul a 500-ton train at 60 miles per hour, but proved capable of reaching a maximum speed of 80 miles per hour in tests.

Following extensive evaluation, New York Central ordered a fleet of 35 similar electrics. But another terrible wreck that occurred shortly after the inauguration of electric service to Grand Central raised questions about the tracking and stability of the T-motors. To avoid further controversy, New York Central decided to replace the guiding pony wheels with more flexible guiding bogey trucks. The rebuilt locomotives featured a 2-D-2 wheel arrangement and were redesignated "S-motors." The prototype was classed S-1, while production locomotives were classed S-2. A few years later, New York Central ordered an additional 12 electrics, classed S-3.

The S-motors were the first electric locomotives equipped for multiple-unit operation. Frank Sprague invented the multiple unit in order to allow a single operator to control more than one electric vehicle. Years later, MU capabilities would prove instrumental in the practical application of the diesel-electric locomotive in America, and on rapid transit trains worldwide. Today nearly all locomotives are so equipped, and it is common to see a locomotive engineer controlling a half dozen locomotives from a single throttle.

In their early years, the S-motors were assigned to all of New York Central's long-distance trains, and coach-hauled suburban trains destined for Grand Central. In later years, as trains grew heavier and longer, more powerful electrics superseded the S-motors in mainline service. However, some of the S-motors were retained for secondary service and switching duties. The design proved extremely durable, and a handful of them survived as switchers until the early 1980s. They were the first, and the last, all-electric locomotives to work the former New York Central third rail territory. Today trains over these lines are either all-electric multiple units, or hauled by "dual-mode" diesel-electric/electrics (specialized diesel locomotives designed to operate using either the third rail or an on-board diesel engine). Several of the pioneering S-motors, including the venerable S-1 prototype, have been preserved.

◄ New York Central's pioneer electric locomotive, S1 No. 100 (originally No. 6000), was still hard at work in the summer of 1961 switching Mott Haven yard. The S-motor electrics spent their entire careers working within the confines of the New York Central's third-rail suburban electrified district.
Richard Jay Solomon

▲ Forlorn and lonely, but not forgotten! Here is another view of old New York Central 100, seen stored south of Albany, New York, in the winter of 1997. This historically significant locomotive has been preserved from scrapping, but as of this writing has not been properly restored.
Brian Solomon

This is a remarkably short time, compared to today when it can take decades of surveys, studies, impact statements, and political discussions to implement existing technology.

New York Central chose a low-voltage, direct current (660 volts) electrification system. Electricity was provided to trains using a specially designed under-running third rail, the very first of its kind. An "under-running third rail" means the contact shoe draws current from the bottom side of the rail, while the top side is covered by protective wooden shielding to minimize the chance of electrocution of people working along the tracks. Initially the electrification only extended to High Bridge in the Bronx, where steam power took over. Under New York Central, electrification was eventually extended to Croton, 33 miles north of Grand Central on the Hudson Division, and to North White Plains on the Harlem Line, along with some branches.

To haul its trains, New York Central first designed a powerful, compact electric locomotive, a machine largely the work of Asa Batchelder. The prototype, built by Alco and General Electric, debuted in 1904. It used a double-ended center design, with four powered axles and guiding pony wheels at each end in a 1-D-1 arrangement. Its four 550-horsepower motors were a state-of-the-art, gearless bipolar design in which the armature was mounted directly on the powered axle, and twin poles were suspended from the frame. Earlier designs used a network of gears to connect the motor and axles. This locomotive, designated Class L, and later Class T,

PENNSYLVANIA GG1

Pennsylvania Railroad's New York to Philadelphia mainline was the heaviest traveled railway line in the United States when this photo was exposed at Frankford Junction in 1959. Here, GG1 No. 4892 leads a mixed consist of heavyweight and streamlined passenger cars. Today this route is part of Amtrak's Northeast Corridor, the route of the Acela Express.
Richard Jay Solomon

PENNSYLVANIA GG1

Pennsylvania Railroad's GG1 electric was synonymous with speed, power, and progress. When the PRR electrified its New York-to-Washington mainline in the 1930s, it was one of the most advanced railway lines in the world. On September 6, 1959, GG1 4887 leads the *Afternoon Keystone*, which used the experimental Budd Tubular Train, at Frankford Junction.
Richard Jay Solomon

LOCOMOTIVE FACTS

RAILROAD:	PENNSYLVANIA RAILROAD
BUILDER:	VARIOUS
MODEL/TYPE:	GG1
WHEEL ARRANGEMENT:	2-C C-2
HORSEPOWER:	4,620
TRACTIVE EFFORT:	NA
YEARS BUILT:	1934-1943

The throaty bark of an airhorn and the accelerating whir of electric motors announced the presence of America's most famous electric locomotive, Pennsylvania's renowned GG1. This distinctive pinstriped, streamlined machine was the pride of Pennsy's acclaimed mainline electrification—by far the most extensive project of its kind in North America. For nearly five decades this magnificent fleet of electrics raced up and down the Northeast Corridor. They outlived the mighty Pennsylvania Railroad, and its ill-fated successor Penn Central, running until 1983. They are still heralded as one of the best electric locomotive designs.

In 1928, Pennsylvania announced its ambitious plans to electrify its heavily trafficked mainline operations between New York City and Washington, D.C., including branches, secondary mainlines, and its namesake mainline from Philadelphia to Harrisburg, Pennsylvania. This was an expansion of its successful Philadelphia suburban electrification, which used a high-voltage alternating current overhead transmission system pioneered by Pennsylvania Railroad's connecting line, New Haven Railroad. Pennsylvania's New York-Washington route was the primary transportation artery connecting America's biggest and most important cities. It accommodated hundreds of long-distance and suburban passenger trains and freight trains daily.

Despite the onset of the Great Depression, PRR went ahead with its ambitious electrification plans, albeit with significant financial assistance from the federal government. The mainline to Washington was opened to electric service in February 1935, and the Harrisburg electrification opened in 1939. Suburban services were largely handled by a vast fleet of Tuscan red, owl-eye multiple units, known as MP54s. Long-distance passenger trains, hourly "Clockers" between New York and Philadelphia, heavy suburban trains, and freight were hauled by electric locomotives. Initially PRR designed a fleet of boxcab electrics using the most successful steam locomotive wheel arrangements of the day, but arranged in a dual-cab bidirectional format.

Several different boxcab designs were built, and the most successful of these were the 2-C-2 P5 and P5a. (As described earlier, wheel-arrangement designations for electric locomotives count axles in truck or bogie groupings; unpowered axles are indicated with numbers, powered ones with letters. This is contrary to steam locomotive wheel arrangement designations, which count wheels, and designate powered wheels by central placement, rather than letters). However, early in their careers, the P5s proved inadequate for high-speed passenger service. Furthermore, a disastrous grade crossing accident demonstrated the dangers of a front-end cab design. As

a result of its experience, PRR decided to design a new class of electric locomotive for its premier services. It built two different prototypes for testing. Both used a streamlined center cab design, but featured very different wheel arrangements. One locomotive, Class R1, had a 2-D-2 arrangement, the same as the successful 4-8-4 Northern type of steam locomotive. The other used a 2-C+C-2 articulated arrangement, based on PRR's experience testing a New Haven EP-3 boxcab with the same setup. This was the GG1 prototype. (The locomotive's class designation was strictly a function of its wheel arrangement. In PRR steam locomotive terms, a G class steam locomotive was a Ten-Wheeler, which used a 4-6-0 wheel arrangement; thus a GG1 was essentially two G locomotives back to back.)

Following extensive testing, the GG1 was deemed the superior locomotive and selected for mass production. The Pennsylvania Railroad hired the industrial designer, Raymond Loewy, to refine the GG1's appearance. Loewy was the most respected man in his

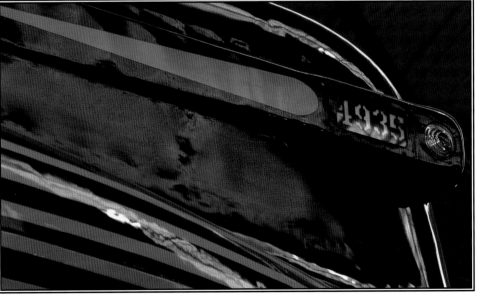

field, having practically invented the profession of industrial design. Although he is frequently solely credited with the GG1's characteristic shape, Loewy was not responsible for the basic design. His primary refinements were the seamless welded skin, instead of the crude riveted skin used on the prototype, and the classy five stripe "cat's whiskers" paint scheme—which would later be adapted as PRR's primary passenger diesel scheme.

Between 1935 and 1943, PRR assembled a fleet of 139 GG1s for service on its electrified lines. They were numbered from 4800 to 4938. Some of the locomotives were built at the railway's renowned Altoona shops, where many of PRR's steam locomotives were built. (The first GG1, No. 4800, the non-Loewy design, is fondly known as "Old Rivets" because of its nonwelded sheet metal.) Others were built by Baldwin, or General Electric. Although they used electrical components from either Westinghouse or General Electric, and were erected at three different locations, the GG1s were essentially a standard design.

Initially they were primarily assigned to premier passenger runs. They featured prominently in advertisements and promotional materials. Perhaps the most famous of all GG1s was the

O-scale Lionel model, owned by tens of thousands of children across the United States.

Originally the GG1 fleet was dressed in the Loewy design scheme—Brunswick green and five gold stripes. In the early 1950s, a few locomotives were painted in PRR's Tuscan red with five gold stripes, a scheme that many consider the G's most attractive dress. In the mid-1950s, PRR adopted a new, simplified paint scheme for the GG1s and other locomotives. A single, broad stripe replaced the five narrow stripes, and a large PRR keystone was painted on the side. A variation of this scheme employed Tuscan red, instead of a very blackish Brunswick green, for the body of the locomotive.

When PRR began retiring many of its older boxcabs, a number of Gs were bumped into freight service. In 1968 the mighty PRR was assimilated by merger with its once archrival, New York Central, into the gargantuan Penn Central. This ill-fated railroad would soon collapse in the abyss of bankruptcy, the worst the world had ever seen. Despite this, and the application of a hideous Spartan black paint scheme, the bulk of the GG1s continued to run. Following the absorption of the bankrupt New Haven Railroad into Penn Central, GG1s ran past New York City for the first time on a regular basis, all

GG1 4872 crosses the Delaware in June 1963. The GG1's tenure spanned nearly five decades from 1934 until 1983. The very last GG1s in regular service were a dozen locomotives assigned to NJ Transit and operated on New York & Long Branch trains between Penn Station and South Amboy. *Richard Jay Solomon*

In June 1963, Pennsylvania Railroad GG1 4917 leads the Seaboard Air Line *Silver Meteor* southbound over the Delaware River at Trenton. The *Silver Meteor* was one of several through trains that operated directly from New York's Penn Station to the southeastern United States. Today Amtrak operates a train by the same name between New York and Florida. *Richard Jay Solomon*

the way to the end of the 11,000 volt AC electrification at New Haven. For a short time they were typical locomotives on the former New Haven Shoreline route. When Amtrak was created in 1971, it inherited a number of GG1s for service on the New Haven to Washington, D.C., Northeast Corridor. Ten years later, they were finally superseded by a more modern locomotive, the Swedish inspired AEM-7 (see page 148).

In 1976, Conrail assumed the freight operations of several bankrupt Northeastern railways, including Penn Central, and inherited a number of freight service Gs, along with other types of former PRR, New York Central, and New Haven electric locomotives. Only one GG1, Rivets, was ever properly painted into Conrail Blue. Conrail discontinued all-electric freight operations a few years after taking over from Penn Central. The last active fleet of GG1s were a few assigned to the New Jersey Department of Transportation (later NJ Transit), operating on New York & Long Branch suburban trains between South Amboy, New Jersey, and Pennsylvania Station, New York. Finally in October 1983, after nearly 50 years of continuous service, the last GG1 lowered its pantograph for the last time. Today, several Gs are preserved in railway museums around the country.

LITTLE JOE ELECTRICS

Built for Russia, the "Little Joes" were named for Soviet dictator Joseph Stalin. The Cold War intervened, as politics have been known to interfere with railroad operations from time to time, and the Little Joes found work in Indiana, Montana, and Brazil. Milwaukee Road's Little Joes spent 24 years moving freight in Montana's Big Sky country. Mel Patrick

LITTLE JOE ELECTRICS

One of the most unusual and most intriguing American railways was Milwaukee Road's famed Pacific Extension, an improbable transcontinental line, completed 40 years after the first American transcon. It traversed the wilds of Montana, Idaho and Washington. Shortly after the turn of the twentieth century, the Chicago, Milwaukee & St. Paul, a prosperous granger line, better known as the Milwaukee Road, was dissatisfied with the service to the coast provided by the James J. Hill-owned Northern Pacific, and Great Northern lines. So it set out to build its own route to the West Coast. This was a bold move, considering that most of the American railway network was in place by that time, and few new lines were being built. Milwaukee's line was completed in 1909, and ran roughly parallel to the Northern Pacific. The Milwaukee had a rough, rock-and-roll profile that surmounted no less than five western mountain ranges, making operations on this route especially tough. Long grades, some consisting of prolonged 2.2 percent climbs, made for slow running, and required lots of power. The cost of transporting coal for locomotive fuel proved a great expense, and Milwaukee began investigating alternatives to steam power.

Milwaukee was inspired by the electrification of the Montana mining road, Butte Anaconda & Pacific, and by nearby Great Northern, which had recently electrified its operations over the Washington Cascades. Based on these successes, Milwaukee made the unprecedented decision to electrify more than 600 miles of its newly constructed Pacific Extension. While railroads had successfully electrified short stretches of line, the vast scope of Milwaukee's plan was unprecedented. It included two very long, but disconnected, electrified segments. Unlike overhead electrification on eastern railroads, which used high voltage alternating current, Milwaukee adopted an overhead system similar to the BA&P's that was energized with 3,000 volts of direct current.

The first electric operations were initiated in 1915, and by 1920 the majority of Milwaukee's electrification was in operation, extending over 647 miles. The first segment stretched 440 miles from Harlowton, Montana, to Avery, Idaho. The second went 207 miles from Othello, Washington, to Tacoma, and was eventually extended to Seattle. At the time of its completion, the Milwaukee Road had the longest, most extensive mainline electrification in the world. It was considered a model for future electrified networks, and inspired railway engineers from Europe and Japan, as well as those in America, to study the possibilities of large-scale electrification. Through electrification, Milwaukee reduced the cost of its day-to-day operation, and greatly speeded up its freight and passenger services.

During the 1920s, other railroads seriously investigated the advantages of electrification. Southern Pacific considered electrifying its heavy mountain operations over Donner Pass, and electric pioneer Pennsylvania drafted plans for electrifying its heavily traveled New York–Philadelphia–Washington mainline. While the PRR completed its project, and several other railroads initiated less-ambitious electrification schemes, American railroads never embraced mainline electrification on a wide scale, despite much contemplation and the long-term economic benefits afforded by electric operations. The extremely high cost of erecting catenary and of building substations and related facilities required far more investment than most American lines were willing to make. While numerous electrification schemes were discussed over the years, ultimately American railroads adopted the diesel-electric as their preferred motive power. Diesels offered many of the same benefits as electrification at a lower initial cost.

In the late 1940s, 30 years after it electrified its Pacific Extension, Milwaukee Road began to dieselize its steam operations. During the steam-to-diesel transition, some railroads also eliminated their electrification systems in an effort to streamline operations. Both the Boston & Maine and the Great Northern abandoned their short electric operations in favor of diesels. While Milwaukee Road investigated discontinuing its electrics at that time, it instead chose another path.

In 1946, the Soviet Union ordered 20 electric locomotives from General Electric. They were 88 feet, 10 inches long, weighed 273 tons, used a 2-D+D-2 articulated wheel arrangement, and generated a whopping 110,750 pounds tractive effort. These massive double-ended streamlined machines were the most powerful

LOCOMOTIVE FACTS	
RAILROAD:	MILWAUKEE ROAD
BUILDER:	GENERAL ELECTRIC
MODEL/TYPE:	"LITTLE JOE"
WHEEL ARRANGEMENT:	2-D D-2
HORSEPOWER:	NA
STARTING TRACTIVE EFFORT:	110, 750 LBS.
YEAR BUILT:	1949

electrics ever built in North America. Soviet railways use a broad gauge—5 feet between the rails, instead of the 4 foot, 8.5 inch standard gauge used in America and most of continental Europe. These electrics were designed for the Soviet broad gauge. During the course of construction, however, international relations between the United States and the Soviet Union broke down and Cold War hostilities began. So before the order could be delivered, General Electric found it needed another buyer. The orphaned electrics were nicknamed "Little Joes," after "Big" Joseph Stalin, the legendary Soviet premier.

In December 1948, Milwaukee Road borrowed one of the Joes for four months of testing on its electrified lines. During the test, Milwaukee was impressed with the machine's tremendous hauling power, and expressed interest in acquiring the whole lot of 20 from GE. General Electric ultimately sold Milwaukee Road just 12 of the "Little Joes," which the railroad modified at its Milwaukee, Wisconsin, shops for service on its lines. Ten were assigned to freight services between Harlowton, Montana, and Avery, Idaho, while the remaining two were equipped with steam boilers for passenger service. They were used to haul Milwaukee's new streamlined *Olympian Hiawatha*. In conjunction with the purchase of the Joes, Milwaukee upgraded its Montana electrification to supply greater amounts of power.

General Electric sold three Joes to a northern Indiana interurban electric line, Chicago, South Shore & South Bend, which operated electrically powered freight and passenger services. These Joes were rewired for operation on South Shore's 1,500-volt DC overhead and assigned to freight service. The five remaining Joes were sold to the Paulista Railway in Brazil.

The Little Joes were significantly more powerful than Milwaukee's 1915-era boxcabs, and they had multiple-unit capability, which permitted Milwaukee Road to assign pairs of them to freight service. The Little Joes could haul twice the tonnage of boxcabs and get over the road significantly faster, too. In the late 1950s, Milwaukee modified the Joes so that it could run them in multiples with diesel-electrics, a unique feature on an American line.

The typical Milwaukee electric freight of the early 1960s was powered by a pair of Joes and a GP9. This new power arrangement permitted Milwaukee to eliminate most helper operations on its Montana lines, producing considerable cost savings.

By the early 1970s, Milwaukee's electrification was showing the signs of age. Once heralded as the epitome of modern railroading, it was now little more than a curious antique. Some of the original boxcabs were still running, and the Little Joes were more than 20 years old. Milwaukee studied the possibility of electrifying the gap between Avery and Othello, but ultimately chose to discontinue its electric operations. The Washington lines succumbed first, while the Avery to Harlowton segment lasted a few more years. Finally in June 1974, Milwaukee operated its last electric freight. The end of electric operations foreshadowed further retrenchment. By the mid-1970s Milwaukee was in deep financial trouble. Its Pacific Extension was flanked by the lines of recently merged Burlington Northern, and the Milwaukee was on the verge of total collapse.

Milwaukee was reorganized in 1980, but many of its lines were abandoned or sold. Milwaukee's fabled Pacific Extension was cut and the rails lifted. Today, visions of Little Joes lifting a heavy freight over Pipestone Pass or negotiating Idaho's sinuous Loop Creek Canyon are just a memory. In some places, the right of way is no longer even visible.

AEM-7

For more than two decades, the AEM-7 has been Amtrak's standard power on the Northeast Corridor. The locomotives have earned several nicknames, including "Swedish Meatballs" and "Mighty Mouse." In September 1989, Amtrak No. 904 leads an eastbound into New Haven, Connecticut. Brian Solomon

AEM-7

The rails sing, there is a vibration in the air, and whoosh, a red, white, and blue locomotive hauling an eight-car silver train blasts by at 125 miles per hour! Is something wrong? Has the train run away? No, it's just Amtrak's *Express Metroliner* from Washington, D.C., to New York's Penn Station.

American designers and engineers were pioneers in the field of electrified railroads. America can take credit for numerous inventions and significant innovations, from multiple-unit control to the first large-scale multitraffic mainline electrified railways. After World War I, many railways were seriously considering large-scale electrification programs. While some of these were undertaken, the enormous initial costs of wiring and power distribution were considered excessive by most carriers. In the mid-1930s, the perfection of the diesel-electric locomotive by General Motor's Electro-Motive Division offered a different "electrification" solution.

Following World War II, the shift in locomotive technology from steam to diesel-electric began on a large scale. Within 15 years, nearly all steam locomotives had been retired in favor of diesels. While less apparent, this shift also ended most interest in conventional electrification schemes, and diesels ultimately displaced many existing electrified lines. Yet American electric locomotive technology continued to evolve through the early 1960s, providing new designs for existing lines. In the early 1960s, the Pennsylvania Railroad ordered a fleet of modern E44 electrics to replace aging 1930 vintage boxcabs, including the P5as. The phenomenal success of the Japanese Shinkansen in the mid-1960s—technology refined from American prototypes—spurred interest in high-speed electric railway technology in the United States. Research sponsored by the federal government resulted in the development of the 125-mile per hour Pennsylvania Railroad *Metroliner* multiple-units. These trains were capable of reaching 164 miles per hour in special tests, but existing track infrastructure and signaling could not maintain such speeds in regular service.

Despite this achievement, the sad state of the railway industry in the late 1960s precluded a serious investment in high-speed railway technology. The merger between the Pennsylvania Railroad and New York Central in 1968, and the inclusion of bankrupt New Haven Railroad in 1969, resulted in a catastrophic financial collapse. One of the results of Penn Central's woes was the creation of the National Railroad Passenger Corporation—better known as Amtrak—by the federal government in 1971. By this time,

▲ On election day in 1992, a pair of AEM-7s race through Newark, Delaware, at about 110 miles per hour toward the nation's capital. Amtrak usually assigns two AEM-7s to trains with more than eight cars. *Brian Solomon*

▼ New Jersey Transit's ALP44s are essentially the same machines as Amtrak's AEM-7s. NJT No. 4424 leads train No. 3263 along the Northeast Corridor at North Rahway, New Jersey. This train will run down the old New York and Long Branch via South Amboy, once the stomping grounds of the Pennsylvania Railroad's famous GG1s. *Patrick Yough*

LOCOMOTIVE FACTS

RAILROAD: AMTRAK AND OTHERS

BUILDER: BUDD AND EMD UNDER LICENSE FROM ASEA

MODEL/TYPE: AEM-7

WHEEL ARRANGEMENT: B-B

HORSEPOWER: 7,000

TRACTIVE EFFORT: NA

YEARS BUILT: STARTING IN 1979

nearly all intercity passenger trains were running at a deficit. Amtrak relieved the railroads, especially Penn-Central, which carried roughly half of America's intercity railroad passengers, of the burden of providing long-distance passenger services. This was a crucial moment in the history of railway passenger travel in the United States. Most American railroads turned over their passenger services to Amtrak on May 1, 1971. While many trains and routes were discontinued overnight, Amtrak maintained a core-passenger network.

The shining star of the new Amtrak empire was the Penn Central Northeast Corridor between Boston, New York, and Washington, D.C. Amtrak continued to work toward higher-speed operation. Initially Amtrak provided passenger services on all of its routes using locomotives and passenger cars inherited from the contributing railroads. However, Amtrak soon ordered a host of new equipment. For its Northeast Corridor, Amtrak ordered a fleet of new electrics from General Electric. These large boxy electrics were designated E60CP, and E60CH, reflecting a difference in train-heating options. They were originally intended for high-speed operation, and designed to supersede the aging GG1 fleet, some of which were approaching 40 years old. Unfortunately they proved inadequate for high-speed operation and were limited to just 85 miles per hour on the mainline. While the E60s remained in passenger service for heavy long-distance services (some were later sold to a private coal carrier, Navajo Mine; others were conveyed to commuter hauler NJ Transit), Amtrak needed to go elsewhere for a new high-speed locomotive design. And despite nearly 70 years of producing innovative electric designs domestically, America swallowed its pride and looked overseas for a state-of-the-art electric locomotive. Following tests in the mid-1970s, Amtrak concluded that the Swedish State Railways (Staten Järnväger, abbreviated SJ) Rc4 electric design—the latest in the Rc series, built by Allmänna Svenska Elektriska Aktiebolag (ASEA)—was the best adapted to its service requirements.

Amtrak could have done worse, as it had picked one of the best locomotives on the market. The Swedish Rc design is acclaimed by several authorities as the world's most successful electric locomotive. It was developed in the 1960s as a dual-service electric, and was the first commercially produced locomotive to employ thyristor motor control. Since its debut, more than 2,000 locomotives based on the Rc design have been built for service in Europe. Today they can be found in daily service in more than a half-dozen nations from Sweden to Bulgaria.

While the Rc4 in service on SJ was designed for freight and passenger service, and intended for a maximum speed of just 84 miles per hour, the variation designed for Amtrak was intended strictly for high-speed passenger service, capable of regular operation up to 125 miles per hour. The newly designed machine, designated AEM-7, was built by General Motor's Electro-Motive Division at La Grange, Illinois. The AEM-7 closely resembles its Swedish prototypes, but has a sturdier body, weighs roughly 17 percent more, and is significantly more powerful. The AEM-7 delivers 53,300 pounds tractive effort, and up to 7,000 horsepower. It is only 51 feet, 5.75 inches long, significantly shorter than most American locomotives. By contrast, an E60 measures 71 feet, 3 inches, and the GG1, 79 feet, 6 inches. Initially Amtrak ordered 47 AEM-7s, which were delivered in the early 1980s. This permitted the immediate retirement of Amtrak's GG1 fleet, and the reassignment of the *Metroliner* MUs. Amtrak later ordered an additional five AEM-7s to replace machines damaged in accidents.

Three commuter agencies (established after Amtrak to relieve private railroads' suburban passenger operations) have followed Amtrak's lead, ordering AEM-7s or similar locomotives for their passenger services. The Philadelphia-based South Eastern Pennsylvania Transportation Authority bought seven AEM-7s for push-pull service. Unlike Amtrak's, these locomotives were assembled by Bombardier. Maryland Rail Commuter Service (known as MARC) has four AEM-7s for its Baltimore-to-Washington service over Amtrak's Northeast Corridor. Beginning in 1990, NJ Transit, which operates a host of suburban services in New Jersey, ordered a variation of the AEM-7, called ALP44, built by ASEA's successors, ABB and Adtranz. As of this writing there are 32 ALP44s for service on the Northeast Corridor and former Delaware, Lackawanna & Western electrified suburban lines.

The successful import of the Rc design set an important precedent of looking overseas for advanced electric railway technology. In the mid-1990s, when Amtrak began to re-explore high-speed development, it tested several successful European high-speed train designs, including the Swedish built X2000. Ultimately it settled on the adaptation and melding of French and Canadian designs for its high-speed *Acela Express* tilting trains.

New Jersey Transit No. 4410 pauses at New Brunswick, New Jersey, with a commuter train bound for New York's Penn Station. Amtrak's AEM-7s were assembled by EMD under license from Swedish manufacturer ASEA, but the ALP44s were built by ASEA's successors, ABB and Adtranz. Both locomotives are close relatives of the Swedish Rc-4, used by many European countries. *Brian Solomon*

ACELA EXPRESS

Prior to the introduction of the Acela Express, Amtrak electrified the segment of the Northeast Corridor between Boston and New Haven. Before then, passenger trains were hauled by traditional diesel-electric locomotives. During the transition from diesel to electric operations, three different types of equipment operated over the line, including trains hauled by 1970s-era F40PH diesels. Brian Solomon

ACELA EXPRESS

Amtrak's *Acela Express* is the fastest regularly scheduled train in North America. It can operate at a top speed of 150 miles per hour on several tangent sections of mainline between Boston and New York. More important than its speed is that the train offers a much higher level of service on the Northeast Corridor than existed previously. *Brian Solomon*

Here's a riddle: What looks like something designed for NASA on the outside, but has European flare and elegance on the inside? It is Amtrak's new *Acela Express*, a modern, high-speed train built for service on the Northeast Corridor between Boston, New York, and Washington. It is the very latest American high-speed train—a wonder to behold and a thrill to ride.

December 11, 2000, dawned cloudy and crisp, yet it was a bright and shining moment for Amtrak. This was the day long awaited, the inaugural run of *Acela Express* between Washington and Boston. By the time the train carried its first passengers, it was already familiar to

a lot of people. A few weeks earlier, on November 16, Amtrak performed a successful demonstration run for the press that was seen on television nationwide. *Acela Express* is the crowning achievement of the Northeast Corridor project. Finally, after years of discussion and planning, Americans were finally able to enjoy high-speed train service. *Acela Express* is not like other American trains, and it marks a bold step ahead for Amtrak. Its interior was the result of extensive studies, looking at European train designs and getting passengers' opinions. The result is a pleasure to ride. It is comfortable, convenient, and fast. *Acela Express* employees are pleasant and courteous, and the train's atmosphere is relaxing.

There are two classes of travel aboard the train: Business and First Class. In both cases passengers are considered "guests" and treated as such. Business Class features two-by-two seating, meaning there are pairs of seats separated by a center aisle. Many of the seats are arranged in sets of four facing one another, with an adjustable table between them. This allows passengers to sit together and share a meal, discuss business, enjoy a board game, or just chat. It is this type of seating that helps distinguish train travel from less comfortable modes. Other seats are separated in pairs and have conventional pull-down tray tables, such as typically found on Amtrak trains and on airplanes. The seats are slightly larger than those used on high-speed trains in Europe and Japan, and in general passengers will find the train remarkably roomy, compared to all other modes of intercity travel. First Class guests are treated to a nice meal and drinks as part of their fare.

A buffet car situated in the middle of the train sells snacks and drinks. Passengers may take these back to their seats, or consume them in the lounge portion of the buffet. The arrangement of this car is remarkably similar to the *Eurostar*, which runs between London, Paris, and Brussels by way of the 31-mile-long Channel Tunnel.

To make *Acela Express* service possible to Boston, Amtrak rehabilitated its line between Boston and New Haven, Connecticut, a route once operated by the old New Haven Railroad. Amtrak

equipped the route with modern high voltage, overhead electrification, similar to that already used west of New Haven to Washington, but using more advanced technology. It also rebuilt tracks for high-speed operations, raising the maximum speed limit on some stretches to 150 miles per hour, the fastest in North America. The combined effect of the high speeds and the elimination of the engine change at New Haven—needed to exchange diesel to electric locomotives—has allowed Amtrak to trim its scheduled time

◄ Amtrak introduced a whole new image along with its new *Acela Express* high-speed service. Unfortunately, considerable confusion has surrounded the use of the Acela name. Only the *Acela Express* trains use the new high-speed tilting electric equipment. Other trains, operated under the marketing name *Acela Regional*, use conventional equipment. *Brian Solomon*

▼ On December 11, 2000, the very first revenue *Acela Express* arrives at New Haven. As is the case with many high-profile railway services, the name of the service has become inseparable from the equipment. In 30 years, when this train set is operating on the Trenton local, will it still be called the *Acela Express*? *Brian Solomon*

LOCOMOTIVE FACTS

RAILROAD: AMTRAK

BUILDER: BOMBARDIER/ALSTOM

MODEL/TYPE: ACELA
EXPRESS POWERCAR

WHEEL ARRANGEMENT: B-B

HORSEPOWER: 6,166

STARTING TRACTIVE EFFORT: NA

YEARS BUILT: 1998 TO PRESENT

between Boston and New York to just 3 hours and 28 minutes, from an earlier schedule of 4 hours and 5 minutes. This has made Amtrak more competitive with airline shuttle services.

Amtrak also has the advantage of directly serving city centers instead of outlying airports. With inner city traffic congestion getting worse everyday, this can make a big difference for travelers.

While airline travel and highway travel is notoriously stressful in the Northeast, Amtrak's *Acela Express* service is nearly stress free.

The New York to Washington running times are slightly faster too, but these do not reflect such a radical improvement as the Boston to New York time because *Acela Express* service only tops 135 miles per hour on this portion of the run, just a little faster than the 125 miles per hour that was already permitted.

Initially just one *Acela Express* train was in service, offering a single high-speed round trip daily. This serv-

ice is augmented by more conventional trains, running on slower schedules. Eventually, as more high-speed trains are put into service, Amtrak will schedule more frequent trips. Amtrak eventually hopes to run 10 daily round trip *Acela Express* trains between Boston and Washington, and even more trains between New York and Washington.

The *Acela Express* is a new train design that melds elements of the French high-speed TGV propulsion technology with a tilting mechanism developed for the Canadian "Light Rapid Comfortable" (LRC) trains in the 1980s. They use state-of-the-art three-phase alternating current traction that enables the train to accelerate to high speeds very quickly, and requires fewer electric motors than old direct current technology. This puts the *Acela* in the same family as most modern high-speed trains in Europe and Japan, which also use three-phase AC propulsion. To the observer, the *Acela* has little in common with big modern coal-hauling diesels, but both of these new types of trains use AC traction (see Electro-Motive Division's SD70MAC, page 118, and General Electric's AC6000CW, page 128).

Acela Express is the first large-scale application of AC propulsion for high-speed rail in North America. The technology was first commercially developed in Germany for moderately high-speed (100- to 125-mile per hour) locomotives in the late 1970s, and later adapted

for use on Germany's InterCity Express high-speed trains in the late 1980s. One of the ICE trains was tested on the Northeast Corridor during 1993 in preparation for Amtrak's own high-speed trains.

Each *Acela Express* train uses a high-horsepower streamlined electric locomotive at each end of a six-car articulated train set—the cars share end trucks and are semi-permanently coupled. Each locomotive can provide up to 6,166 continuous horsepower, giving the train a total of 12,332 horsepower. That's a lot of power for a six-car passenger train. It is more horsepower than three EMD SD70MACs used to haul a 12,000-ton coal train across Wyoming. However, high horsepower is needed for rapid acceleration and to maintain continuous high speeds.

The tilting body allows for faster operation through curves without the need for massive changes in the existing railway infrastructure. Tilting reduces the unpleasant pulling effects of centrifugal forces on passengers, making for a more comfortable ride. The effect is amazing, and it is so subtle when riding along at speed, that one hardly even notices the train tilting into curves. In addition to the LRC trains in Canada, a number of European trains use tilting mechanisms. These include the Swedish X2000, which was also tested on the Northeast Corridor in 1992–1993; German ICT; Italian "Pendolino"; and the latest generation of

Spanish Talgo trains, some of which are now in medium-speed Amtrak service on the West Coast.

Acela Express trains are assembled by a consortium of Bombardier and Alstom at Barre, Vermont, with some final work being performed in New York State. Amtrak has ordered 20 six-car trains, and these were still under construction as of this writing, in December 2000. The advent of *Acela Express* is one of the most innovative and exciting developments in American passenger railroading since the first diesel-electric streamliners in the 1930s. Hopefully it will usher in a new age in passenger transport.

The *Acela Express* began with minimal fanfare on December 11, 2000. A subtle congratulations on the train arrival board reminds passengers of the historic event in progress. *Brian Solomon*

Time	Number	Train	To	From	Status	Tr
9:27	2150	ACELA EXPRESS	BOSTON	WASHINGTON	ON TIME	
9:23	1508	METRO-NORTH	NEW HAVEN	GRAND CENTRAL	ON TIME	
9:25	495	N. EAST DIRECT	NEW HAVEN	SPRINGFIELD	ON TIME	
9:29	1549	METRO-NORTH	GRAND CENTRAL	NEW HAVEN	ON TIME	
9:43	95	N. EAST DIRECT R	NEWPORT NEWS	BOSTON	ON TIME	
10:00	1510	METRO-NORTH	NEW HAVEN	GRAND CENTRAL	ON TIME	
10:06	1551	METRO-NORTH	GRAND CENTRAL	NEW HAVEN	ON TIME	

CONGRATULATIONS AMTRAK ON THIS HISTORIC DAY-SERVICE OF AMERICAS FIRST HIGH SPEED TRAIN - ACELA EXPRESS

BIBLIOGRAPHY

Books

Alexander, Edwin P. *Iron Horses.* New York, 1941.

Alexander, Edwin P. *American Locomotives.* New York, 1950.

Alymer-Small, Sidney. *The Art of Railroading.* Vol. VIII. Chicago, 1908.

Anderson, Norman E., and C. G. MacDermot. *PA4 Locomotives.* Burlingame, Calif., 1978.

Armstrong, John H. *The Railroad: What It Is, What It Does.* Omaha, Neb. 1982.

Bruce, Alfred W. *The Steam Locomotive in America.* New York, 1952.

Burch, Edward P. *Electric Traction for Railway Trains.* New York, 1911.

Bush, Donald J. *The Streamlined Decade.* New York, 1975.

Churella, Albert J. *From Steam to Diesel.* Princeton, N.J., 1998.

Comstock, Henry B. *The Iron Horse.* New York, 1971.

Condit, Carl. *Port of New York*, Vols. 1 & 2. Chicago, 1980, 1981.

Conrad, J. David. *The Steam Locomotive Directory of North America*, Volumes 1 & 2. Polo, Ill., 1988.

Diemer, Hugo. *Self-Propelled Railway Cars.* Chicago, 1910.

Dolzall, Gary W., and Stephen F. Dolzall. *Baldwin Diesel Locomotives.* Milwaukee, 1984.

Drury, George H. Guide to North American Steam Locomotives. Waukesha, Wis., 1993.

Dubin, Arthur D. *More Classic Trains.* Milwaukee, 1974.

Farrington, S. Kip, Jr. *Railroads at War.* New York, 1944.

Farrington, S. Kip, Jr. *Railroading the Modern Way.* New York, 1951.

Forney, M. N. *Catechism of the Locomotive.* New York, 1876.

Garmany, John B. *Southern Pacific Dieselization.* Edmonds, Wash., 1985.

Garrett, Colin. *The World Encyclopedia of Locomotives.* London, 1997.

General Motors. *Electro-Motive Division Operating Manual No. 2300.* La Grange, Ill., 1945(?).

Gregg, Newton K. *Train Shed Cyclopedia No. 20.* Novato, Calif., 1974.

Harlow, Alvin F. *The Road of the Century.* New York, 1947.

Haut, F. J. G. *The Pictorial History of Electric Locomotives.* Cranbury, N.J., 1970.

Herrick, Albert B. *Practical Electric Railway Hand Book.* New York, 1906.

Hofsommer, Don L. *Southern Pacific 1900–1985.* College Station, Tex., 1986.

Jennison, Brian, and Victor Neves. *Southern Pacific Oregon Division.* Mukilteo, Wash., 1997.

Kalmbach, A. C. *Railroad Panorama.* Milwaukee, 1944.

Keilty, Edmund. *Interurbans Without Wires.* Glendale, Calif., 1979.

Kiefer, P. W. *A Practical Evaluation of Railroad Motive Power.* New York, 1948.

Kirkland, John F. *The Diesel Builders, Vols. I, II, and III.* Glendale, Calif., 1983.

Kirkland, John F. *Dawn of the Diesel Age.* Pasadena, Calif., 1994.

Klein, Maury. *Union Pacific, Vol. II.* New York, 1989.

Kratville, William, and Harold E. Ranks. *Motive Power of the Union Pacific.* Omaha, Neb., 1958.

Marre, Louis A. *Rock Island Diesel Locomotives.* Cincinnati, Ohio, 1982.

Marre, Louis A. *Diesel Locomotives: The First 50 Years.* Waukesha, Wis., 1995.

Marre, Louis A., and Jerry A. Pinkepank. *The Contemporary Diesel Spotter's Guide.* Milwaukee, 1985.

Middleton, William D. *When the Steam Railroads Electrified.* Milwaukee, 1974.

Middleton, William D. *Grand Central . . . the World's Greatest Railway Terminal.* San Marino, Calif., 1977.

Morgan, David P. *Steam's Finest Hour.* Milwaukee, 1959.

Mulhearn, Daniel J., and John R. Taibi. *General Motors' F-Units.* New York, 1982.

Pinkepank, Jerry A. *The Second Diesel Spotter's Guide.* Milwaukee, 1973.

Ransome-Wallis, P. *World Railway Locomotives.* New York, 1959.

Reagan, H. C., Jr. *Locomotive Mechanism and Engineering.* New York, 1894.

Reck, Franklin M. *On Time.* Electro-Motive Division of General Motors, 1948.

Reck, Franklin M. *The Dilworth Story.* New York, 1954.

Rose, Joseph R. *American Wartime Transportation.* New York, 1953.

Signor, John R. *Tehachapi.* San Marino, Calif. 1983.

Signor, John R. *Donner Pass: Southern Pacific's Sierra Crossing.* San Marino, Calif. 1985.

Signor, John R. *The Los Angeles and Salt Lake Railroad Company.* San Marino, Calif. 1988.

Sillcox, Lewis K. *Mastering Momentum.* New York, 1955.

Sinclair, Angus. *Development of the Locomotive Engine.* New York, 1907.

Solomon, Brian. *Trains of the Old West.* New York, 1998.

Solomon, Brian. *The American Steam Locomotive.* Osceola, Wis., 1998.

Solomon, Brian. *The American Diesel Locomotive.* Osceola, Wis., 2000.

Staff, Virgil. *D-Day on the Western Pacific.* Glendale, Calif., 1982.

Staufer, Alvin F. *New York Central's Early Power, 1831–1916.* Medina, Ohio, 1967.

Staufer, Alvin F. *Pennsy Power III.* Medina, Ohio, 1968.

Staufer, Alvin F., and Edward L. May. *New York Central's Later Power, 1910–1968.* Medina, Ohio, 1981.

Strapac, Joseph A. *Southern Pacific Motive Power Annual 1971.* Burlingame, Calif., 1971.

Strapac, Joseph A. *Southern Pacific Review 1981.* Huntington Beach, Calif., 1982.

Strapac, Joseph A. *Southern Pacific Review 1953–1985.* Huntington Beach, Calif., 1986.

Swengel, Frank M. *The American Steam Locomotive: Volume 1, Evolution.* Davenport, Iowa, 1967.

Westing, Fredrick. *The Locomotives That Baldwin Built.* Seattle, 1966.

White, John H., Jr. *A History of the American Locomotive.* Toronto, 1968.

White, John H., Jr. *Early American Locomotives.* Toronto, 1972.

Brochures

Alco-Méditerranée S.A.R.L. Alco 251 Diesels. Paris, France .

General Electric. GE Locomotives.

Periodicals

Locomotive & Railway Preservation. Waukesha, Wis. (No longer published)

Official Guide to the Railways. New York.

RailNews. Waukesha, Wis. (No longer published)

Railroad History (formerly *Railway and Locomotive Historical Society Bulletin*). Boston, Mass.

Railway Gazette, 1870–1908. New York.

Southern Pacific Bulletin. San Francisco. (No longer published)

Trains. Waukesha, Wis.

Vintage Rails. Waukesha, Wis. (No longer published)

INDEX

0-6-0 Switcher, 28–31
Advisory Mechanical Committee, 34
Alco, 11, 18, 26, 34, 36, 44, 45, 54, 64, 65, 68, 69, 72, 73, 81, 87–89, 98, 100, 106, 126, 137
    Alco "S" Switchers, 62–65
    Alco C-430, 98
    Alco Century Line, 98, 99
    Alco FA, 69
    Alco PA, 41, 74–77
    Alco PB, 76
    Alco RS-1, 68
    Alco RS-2, 68
    Alco RS-3, 66, 69
Alco-Schenectady, 26, 38
Algoma Central, 82
Allmänna Svenska Elektriska Aktiebolag (ASEA), 151
American Freedom Train, 49
American Standard type, 12, 14, 15
Amtrak, 141, 143, 151–157
    Acela Express, 8, 132, 133, 139, 151–157
    Adirondack, 76, 77
    AEM-7, 132, 148–151
    AEM-7 No. 904, 148
    AEM-7 No. 915, 133
    Express Metroliner, 150
    FL9, 9
    Floridian, 65
    GG1, 151
Atlantics, 76
Baldwin Locomotive Works, 18, 26, 31, 52, 54, 55, 65, 68, 77, 80, 81, 88, 89, 93, 126, 142
    Baldwin Shark, 70–73
    Baldwin Shark RF16, 73
Baltimore & Ohio, 18, 44, 52, 73, 122, 136
Bangor & Aroostook, 60
    Bangor & Aroostook No. 42, 60
Batchelder, Asa, 137
Battenkill Railroad RS-3 605, 67, 68
Berkshire, 18, 40, 41, 130
Bernet, John J., 34
Blount, Nelson, 18, 19
Blue Mountain & Reading, 49
Bombardier, 54, 98, 151
Boston & Albany, 10, 34, 37, 41, 111, 130
    B&A J-2c Hudson 619, 40
Boston & Maine, 34, 65, 69, 83, 89, 93, 133, 146
    B&M 0-6-0 No. 427, 9
    B&M Class B-15 Mogul, 16–19
    B&M G-10 No. 723, 30

B&M GP40 No. 314, 93
B&M GP40 No. 340, 95
B&M *Lebanon* No. 187, 15
B&M Mogul No. 1401, 16, 17
B&M Mogul No. 1455, 18
B&M Mogul No. 1496, 19
B&M *Old Maud*, 44
Boston Line, 110–113, 130
Bruce, Alfred, 18, 26
Brunel, Isambard K., 126
Buffalo, Rochester & Pittsburgh, 92
Bullard, William, 30
Burkhardt, Ed, 126
Burlington Northern, 107, 110, 116, 117, 121–123, 130
    BN No. 21, 61
    BN SD70MAC No. 9529, 119
    BNSF DASH 9 No. 1116, 116
    BNSF DASH 9-44CW, 9
    BNSF SD70MAC No. 8955, 123
    Zephyr, 41
Butte Anaconda & Pacific, 146
Campbell, Henry R., 14
Canadian National Railway, 28, 48, 100
    CN No. 2034, 98
Canadian Pacific Railway, 8, 15, 100, 130
    CP *Jupiter*, 14
    CP M-630 No. 4571, 98
Cape Breton & Central Nova Scotia, 97, 100
    CB&CNS No. 305, 97
    CB&CNS No. 2003, 99
    CB&CNS No. 2029, 101
    CB&CNS No. 2032, 97
Cartier Railway, 101
    Cartier Railway C-636 No. 79, 99
Catechism of the Locomotive, 23
Central Railroad of New Jersey, 48, 54, 76
Central Vermont, 81
    CV GP9, 83
    CV No. 8081, 55
Chesapeake & Ohio
    C&O Allegheny, 45
    C&O F7A, 58
    C&O J-3a, 11
Chicago & North Western, 114, 130, 131
    C&NW DASH 9-44CW, 114
    C&NW R-1, 11, 24–27
    C&NW R-1 No. 894, 26
    C&NW R-1 No. 1385, 11, 25, 26, 27
Chicago, South Shore & South Bend, 146, 147
    South Shore No. 802, 146
City of San Francisco, 77
Conrail, 69, 110, 111, 113, 116, 131, 133, 142, 143

Conrail C30-7A, 113
Conrail C32-8, 113
Conrail No. 6579, 110
Conway Scenic Railroad, 28
Cooper-Bessemer, 87, 88
CSX, 113, 130, 131
    CSX AC6000CW No. 613, 55
    CSX AC6000CW No. 673, 130
Delaware & Hudson, 67, 69, 73, 76, 77, 100
    D&H PA No. 16
    D&H PA-1 No. 18, 76
    D&H RF16 No. 1205, 71
Delaware, Lackawanna & Western, 27
Denver & Rio Grande Western, 107
Deutsche Bundesbahn, 122
Deutz MWM, 131
Dilworth, Dick, 80
Dreyfuss, Henry, 41
Duluth, Missabe & Iron Range, 73
Electro-Motive Division, 45, 52, 54–61, 64, 68, 72, 73, 76, 87, 88, 98, 110, 111, 116, 130, 150, 151
    EMD Class 59, 127
    EMD Class 66, 124–127
    EMD Dash-2, 95
    EMD E7, 41
    EMD E-units, 50, 76, 77
    EMD F2, 59
    EMD F3, 59, 60
    EMD F7, 60
    EMD F7A, 60
    EMD F9, 60, 61
    EMD FL9, 57
    EMD FP7, 59
    EMD FT, 18, 45, 58–60
    EMD F-units, 8, 57–61, 69
    EMD GP7, 69, 83
    EMD GP9, 55, 78–83
    EMD GP30, 89
    EMD GP35, 89, 95
    EMD GP40, 91–95
    EMD SD40, 110
    EMD SD40-2, 123
    EMD SD45, 99
    EMD SD70MAC, 118–123, 130, 156, 157
    EMD Tunnel Motors, 102–107
Elgin, Joliet & Eastern, 73
English Electric
    Deltic, 126
    Type 3, Class 37, 126
English Welsh & Scottish Railway, 126, 127
    EW&S No. 66029, 124
    EW&S No. 66240, 127

Erie-Lackawanna, 37, 77
    E-L No. 2527, 87
    E-L PA, 74
    E-L RS-3 No. 1051, 69
    E-L U25B, 86
Erie Railroad, 15, 34, 36, 69
Escanaba & Lake Superior, 73
Eureka & Palisade *Eureka*, 12
Fairbanks-Morse, 54, 68, 81, 88, 93
Fales, Bruce, 15
Fitchburg Railroad, 18
Flatland Illinois Central, 34
Forney, Matthias N., 22
Forney Classification System, 10
Forney Tank, 20–23
Forney Transportation Museum, 27
Fort Wayne Historical Society, 34
General Electric, 54, 55, 68, 73, 93, 98, 101, 106, 137, 142, 147
    GE AC4400CW, 55, 130, 131
    GE AC6000CW, 128–131, 156
    GE C30-7, 123
    GE C30-7A, 9, 108–113
    GE C36-7 No. 6331, 108
    GE DASH 7, 110, 116
    GE DASH 8, 113, 116, 117
    GE DASH 9, 114–117, 131
    GE DASH 9-44CW, 55
    GE U25B, 84–89, 94, 95
    GE U25C, 89, 110
    GE U30C, 110
General Motors, 54, 58, 59, 76, 82, 98, 116, 126, 150, 151
Genesee & Wyoming Alco S-4, 62
German ICT, 157
Gornergrat Railway, 120
Grand Trunk Railway, 28, 83
    Grand Trunk GP9 No. 4557, 82
Grand Trunk Western, 81
Great Northern, 121, 133, 146
Green Mountain Railway No. 302, 94
Guilford Rail System, 67, 92
Gulf, Mobile & Ohio Railroad, 77
Hadley, Ryder & Pedersen, 71, 73
Hale, Robert, 45
Harte, Bret, 14
Hiawathas, 76
Hill, James J., 146
Illinois Central, 48
Ingersoll-Rand, 54, 64, 68, 76, 87
Jervis, John B., 14
Judah, Theodore, 105
Kiefer, Paul, 40
Kratville, William, 45
Krauss-Maffei, 106

Kuhler, Otto, 64
Lackawanna Ten-Wheeler No. 1061, 25
Lehigh & Hudson River Railroad, 73
Lehigh Valley, 69, 73, 77
    Lehigh Valley RS-2 No. 214, 73
Lima, 11, 18, 34, 36, 37, 41, 130
Little Joe Electrics, 144–147
Loewy, Raymond, 52, 53, 71, 73, 141, 142
    Loewy T1 Duplex, 71
Maine Central, 82, 89
    Maine Central GP9 No. 450, 82
    Maine Central U25B No. 229, 89
    Maine Central U25B No. 238, 84, 87
Mallet, 44, 107, 130
Manchester Locomotive Works, 14, 18, 30
Maryland Rail Commuter Service
    (MARC), 151
Massachusetts Bay Transportation
    Authority (MBTA), 77
Mid-Continent Railway Museum, 26, 27
Middleton, William D., 11, 146
Mikado, 18, 34, 49, 52
Milwaukee Road, 76, 78, 126, 133, 146,
    147
    Milwaukee Road No. 263, 132
    Milwaukee Road *Olympian*
Hiawatha, 147
Missouri Pacific, 110
Mogul, 26
Mohawk, 76
Monongahela Railway, 72, 73
Montreal Locomotive Works, 54, 64, 65, 69
    MLW M-640, 100
    MLW Six-Motor Locomotives,
    96–101
Morrison-Knudsen, 54, 69, 77, 89
National Railroad Passenger Corporation,
    150
New Haven Railroad, 9, 30, 60, 69, 77,
    133, 136, 142, 150
    New Haven EP-3, 141
    New Haven *Yankee Clipper*, 77
New Jersey Central, 69
New Jersey Department of Transportation,
    143
New Jersey Transit, 143, 151
    NJ Transit ALP44, 150, 151
    NJ Transit No. 3263, 150
    NJ Transit No. 4410, 151
    NJ Transit No. 4424, 150
New York & Long Branch, 143

New York Central, 10, 26, 34, 37, 53, 64,
    67, 69, 72, 73, 76, 87, 89, 92, 95,
    131, 133, 142, 150
    New York Central A1b No. 1435, 37
    New York Central Class L, 137
    New York Central Class T, 137
    New York Central Hudson, 15,
    38–41, 76
    New York Central Hudson No. 5281, 10
    New York Central J-1b No. 5210, 40
    New York Central J-1c No. 5401, 38
    New York Central J-3a, 11
    New York Central J-3a No. 5344, 41
    New York Central J-3a No. 5411, 40
    New York Central Niagara, 49, 53, 76
    New York Central No. 38, 40
    New York Central No. 5200, 41
    New York Central No. 6000, 133
    New York Central RF16 Shark, 72
    New York Central S-1, 137
    New York Central S-1 No. 858, 64
    New York Central S-2, 137
    New York Central S2 No. 112, 135
    New York Central S-Motor, 134–137
    The Missourian, 40
    Twentieth Century Limited, 40, 65
New York Central & Hudson River
    Railroad *Empire State Express*, 14
New York Elevated Railroad No. 39, 22
Nickel Plate Road, 34, 36
    Nickel Plate Road Berkshire, 11, 15,
    33–37
    Nickel Plate Road No. 741, 33
    Nickel Plate Road No. 759, 37
    Nickel Plate Road No. 765, 34, 36,
    37
    Nickel Plate Road No. 779, 36
Norfolk & Western, 37, 48, 53, 89, 133
Norfolk Southern, 37, 113, 116, 117, 131
Northern, 76, 141
Northern Pacific, 11, 48, 146
Overland Limited, 77
Pacific, 18, 40, 52
"Pendolino," 157
Penn Central, 142, 143, 151
    Penn Central No. 4715, 132
Pennsylvania Railroad, 15, 26, 40, 48, 49,
    52, 69, 80, 83, 88, 133, 150
    Afternoon Keystone, 140
    Metroliner, 150
    PRR Class R1, 141

PRR D16b, 15
PRR GG1, 41, 133, 138–143
PRR GG1 No. 4800, 142
PRR GG1 No. 4872, 143
PRR GG1 No. 4887, 140
PRR GG1 No. 4892, 139
PRR GG1 No. 4917, 143
PRR GG1 No. 4935, 141
PRR GP9, 80
PRR RS-3 No. 8445, 69
PRR T1, 15, 50–53
PRR T1 Duplex, 10, 73
PRR T1 No. 5502, 53
PRR T1 No. 5517, 53
PRR T1 No. 5535, 50
PRR T1 No. 5770, 73
Trailblazer, 50
Pere Marquette, 36
Philadelphia & Reading, 48
Philadelphia & Western Bullet Cars, 41
Philadelphia, Germantown & Norristown
    Railway, 14
Pittsburgh & Lake Erie RS-3 No. 8357, 67
Rail America, 100
Railroad and Engineering Journal, 23
RailTex, 100
Railway Gazette, 23
Ramsdell, Alice, 20
Ramsdell, Frank, 20
Reading Company, 48
    Reading I-10sa 2-8-0 Consolidation,
    48, 49
    Reading T-1, 46–49
    Reading T-1 No. 2102, 46, 48, 49
    Reading T-1 No. 2124, 49
Rhode Island Locomotive Works, 15
Richmond, Fredricksburg & Potomac, 37
Rio Grande, 103
    Rio Grande SD40T-2, 103, 106
Rochester & Southern GP40, 92
Rocket, 44
Rock Island
    Rock Island FP7 No. 410, 59
    Rock Island GP35, 88
    Rock Island U25B, 88
Sandy River & Rangeley Lakes, 20
Santa Fe Railway, 11, 18, 48, 58, 76, 77,
    107, 116, 117, 123, 130
Schenectady Locomotive Works, 18, 26, 87
Seaboard Air Line *Silver Meteor*, 143
Seaboard Coast Line Alco S-2 No. 50, 65

Shinkansen, 132, 150
Siemens AG, 123
Soo Line, 126
South Eastern Pennsylvania
    Transportation Authority, 151
Southern Pacific, 18, 54, 73, 77, 103, 106,
    107, 130, 131
    SP DASH9, 54
    SP Daylight, 49
    SP GP9E 3821, 80EMD NW5, 81
    SP MERVM, 107
    SP SD40, 105
    SP SD45, 88, 107
    SP SD45T-2, 105
    SP SD45T-2 No. 6794, 104
    SP SD45X, 107
    SP Tunnel Motor No. 6770, 107
Sprague, Frank, 136, 137
Stalin, Joseph, 145
Steam Locomotive in America, The, 18, 26
Steamtown, 25, 27, 31, 37
Stephenson, Robert, 44
Swedish State Railways, 151
Talgo, 157
Transcontinental Railroad, 14, 73, 105
Union Pacific, 44, 45, 65, 76, 83, 87, 89,
    93, 106, 107 , 121, 130, 131
    Big Boy, 8, 10, 42–45, 76
    Big Boy No. 4005, 42
    Big Boy No. 4007, 44
    Big Boy No. 4010, 45
    Challenger, 44, 45, 76
    Streamliner, 41
    UP No. 119, 14
Virginian, 37, 133
War Production Board, 52, 59, 64, 72, 76
Western & Atlantic *General*, 14
Western Maryland, 37, 48
Westinghouse, 64, 73, 142
Whyte Classification System, 10
Wilgus, William, 136
Winans, Ross, 23
Wisconsin & Southern, 27
Wisconsin Central, 27, 54, 126, 127
    Wisconsin Central GP40, 91
Woodard, Will, 34
Wylie, Lawrence, 132
Yeoman, Foster, 127
Zapf, Norman, 41